JESUS
VS.
CAESAR

Other Books in the VS. Series

Calvin vs. Wesley by Don Thorsen

Barnabas vs. Paul by C. K. Robertson

Luther vs. Pope Leo by Paul R. Hinlicky

JOERG RIEGER

JESUS VS. CAESAR

FOR PEOPLE TIRED OF SERVING THE WRONG GOD

![Abingdon Press]

Nashville

JESUS VS. CAESAR:
FOR PEOPLE TIRED OF SERVING THE WRONG GOD

Copyright© 2018 by Abingdon Press

This book is printed on acid-free paper.

Library of Congress Cataloging-in-Publication Data has been requested.

978-1-5018-4267-2

Unless otherwise noted all scripture quotations are from the New Revised Standard Version Bible, copyright © 1989 National Council of the Churches of Christ in the United States of America. Used by permission. All rights reserved worldwide. http://nrsvbibles.org/

18 19 20 21 22 23 24 25 26 27—10 9 8 7 6 5 4 3 2 1
MANUFACTURED IN THE UNITED STATES OF AMERICA

To those who are moved, keep moving,
and move others.

CONTENTS

CONTENTS

ACKNOWLEDGMENTS

This book is the result of long and deep engagements with Christianity not only as a faith tradition but as a way of life, and it reflects insights gained by authoring and editing more than twenty books. I greatly appreciate my fellow travelers, in particular those engaged in grassroots movements who have shaped my thinking. Many friends, colleagues, and students have made contributions as well, sometimes by spelling out challenges and disagreements, sometimes by thinking ahead. Those who have engaged this project include Santiago Slabodsky, David Teel, Barbara Wendland, Zachary Settle, and Donna Whitney; conversations with Jeremy Posadas and Rosemarie Henkel-Rieger are also reflected. Thanks also to the colleagues of the Workgroup on Contemporary Theology, with whom I have worked for almost two decades; to the participants in the Class, Religion, and Theology unit at the American Academy of Religion; and to my colleagues at Vanderbilt University who are committed to making a difference both in the church and in the world.

PREFACE

Who doesn't find certain images of God aggravating, annoying, or depressing? Who hasn't felt concern that religion and the church might be headed in the wrong direction? And who doesn't tire of much prevailing God talk because it is either aloof or repressive?

The truth is that worshiping and serving the wrong god has done tremendous damage to people and the earth, and has even led to killing and death. This is the struggle of Jesus vs. Caesar that today is taking place within Christianity itself and that is the topic of this book.

In the history of Christianity, many have died because people worshipped a god of servitude who sanctioned slavery; a god of violence who endorsed torture, mass killings, and war; or a god of privilege who underwrote the "superiority" of white people, straight people, men, or privileged elites at the expense of everyone else. These are only a few of the most detrimental images of God. Others include a god who embodies unilateral power that allows no human agency, blatant insensitivity in the face of suffering, or smothering love that leaves no room to breathe—the power, the insensitivity, and the love of empire.

Many of these challenges were familiar to Jesus, whose concern was serving the true God, a God of life rather than a god of death. In this mission he found many allies in his own Jewish traditions and in the popular religious expressions of his time. But Jesus also experienced conflict with and pushback from those who represented the interests of empire and its gods; so religious and political power brokers decided to get rid of him early on in his ministry (Mark 3:6).

The story of Jesus told in the Gospels is one of emotions flying high on all sides, but siding with the God of life rather than the god of death is worth a good fight. This sort of God talk is no longer aggravating, annoying, or depressing, and it certainly is not boring. When done well, God talk can be life-giving, resisting suffering and death, and potentially providing happier lives for people and the planet. This is what keeps me writing theology after all these years, and what is bound to keep inviting people into the conversation.

Imagine what real conversations about matters of life and death might do for communities of faith—and for the large numbers of people who may not have abandoned their faith but who have left faith communities precisely because they appear to be worshipping and serving the wrong god.

LIFE AND DEATH

Matters of life, death, and inequality have been with us for centuries but are today becoming more pronounced than ever, often related to religious convictions: countless killed by misdirected religious fervor in crusades, ethnic cleansing, and concentration camps; children starving to death because they and their parents are considered second-class human beings; young black men and women shot in the streets for little or no cause; people perishing behind closed doors due to lack of care (especially health care); and ever more rampant forms of inequality. Too much of this is somehow justified and perhaps even propped up by elitist, power-worshipping ideas of God.

Of course, in a postmodern world many would argue that attention to the kinds of tensions and dichotomies that will be addressed in this book is somehow overblown or outdated.[1] There are never just two sides to an issue—the postmodernist argument goes—and we never just find ourselves on one side or another. Complexity is the mantra. Others, considering themselves down-to-earth realists, would add to this conversation that the truth is not found in either of the extremes but somewhere in the middle.

Yet there are dichotomies and challenges (choose this, not that; take sides) in Jesus's message, and they are rooted not just in theology or ideology but in the experience of severe pressures and conflict. In a world of stark inequalities and conflict that amount to matters of life and death, we need to take another look at the conflicts at the heart of everyday life. For the writer of the book of Deuteronomy, life and death hinge on serving the right God: "Today," the voice of Moses intones, "I have set before you life and death" (Deut 30:19).

WAS CAESAR REALLY THAT BAD?

Some might feel that the contrast between Jesus and Caesar, which is the subject of this book, is overblown. Didn't the Roman Empire support the spread of Christianity and help it grow? The roads on which the Apostle Paul traveled were designed by the Romans. The cities in which Christianity first spread were dominated by the Romans. Roman institutions preserved and enhanced the cultures of the ancient world on which most of Western civilization was built. And the *Pax Romana*, the peace established by Roman dominance, created a certain stability. So, can we simply brush off our indebtedness to Rome and Caesar? What might be the problem when Caesar did some good (aqueducts, architecture, and art)?

Whether or not there is a problem depends on how we interpret the tensions experienced by Jesus and the early Christians that are the subject of this book. Why would religious and government officials conspire to get rid of Jesus early on during his ministry (Mark 3:6)? Who killed Jesus and by what means, and who might have had an interest in his death? Why did Paul spend so much of his ministry in prison? Were these tensions all based on misunderstandings—or were they based on some deeper understanding of what Jesus stood for?

Similar conversations can be imagined when people discuss capitalism today, the economic system that dominates the globe. The question is not whether its track record is all bad or all good (too many conversations get stuck there); rather, the question is how we put to use its benefits (the church fathers sometimes referenced Exodus 12:36, "plunder[ing] the Egyptians") and how we negotiate its tensions. Another question is to whom or to what people of faith pledge their allegiance when God and mammon are in contradiction, as they usually are. That is what is at stake when we ask, "Jesus or Caesar?"

INTRODUCTION

THE FUNDAMENTAL TENSION

There is a fundamental tension at the heart of Christianity that existed since its earliest beginnings and has been with us ever since. But this tension is rarely understood. It is not between religion and atheism or between the sacred and the secular, as is commonly assumed. Neither is it between religion and spirituality (as the "spiritual but not religious" crowd might think), nor is it between Christianity and Judaism (another common misunderstanding!), or even between Christianity and other religions.[1]

The tension at the heart of Christianity is located deep within Christianity itself because it is a radical conflict between different forms of Christian faith: it is the tension between faith that is life-giving for all—not just a few—and faith that is not. The tension is between one kind of sacred and another kind of sacred, between one set of religious traditions and another set. And, since faith and religion are always embodied, we are also talking about the tension between some ways of life and others.[2]

> The tension at the heart of Christian faith is the tension between ways of life that are life-giving for all—not just a few—and ways of life that are not.

In this book, this is the tension between Jesus and Caesar. This tension is not a minor one, as we shall see, but amounts to a matter of life

1

and death. Caesar's power is manifest in the conquests of the Roman Empire, which include not only military power but also cultural and religious forces of domination that can be quite subtle at times but that determine the difference between winners and losers. Moreover, Caesar's power, which is the power of empire, affects not only politics and economics but also impacts everything else, including our innermost feelings and our most deeply held religious beliefs.

This means that not even our most cherished images of Jesus are safe from the ruses of empire. For two thousand years, empires—conglomerates of power that seek to control all of life—have shaped Christian ways of thinking about Jesus, often unconsciously.[3] The good news, however, is that no empire has ever been able to take over Christianity completely, and there have been contested and persisting images of Jesus that have continued to inspire alternative ways of life, not only in religion but also in politics and economics. This is the positive side of the story that this book will tell.[4]

This tension between life-giving and malignant forms of religion is deeply rooted in the Jewish traditions. The Hebrew prophets were gravely concerned about certain embodiments of the Jewish religion that resulted in injustice and oppression. The prophet Isaiah hears the voice of God pronouncing judgment: "You serve your own interest on your fast day, and oppress all your workers" (Isa 58:3). Life-giving embodiments of Jewish religion, the prophets remind us, will loosen "the bonds of injustice" (58:6), while malignant religion strikes "with a wicked fist" (58:4).

The prophet Amos has God accuse the faithful of trampling on the poor and taking levies of grain from them (Amos 5:11) and pushing aside the needy in the courts (Amos 5:11-12). The problem has to do with misguided or distorted religion rather than with the absence of religion, for God concludes: "I hate, I despise your festivals, and I take no delight in your solemn assemblies. Even though you offer me your burnt offerings and grain offerings, I will not accept them. . . . Take away from me the noise of your songs" (Amos 5:21-23).

Early forms of Christian faith embodied this tension between life-giving and malignant religion as they found themselves within an empire that was also religious. But why would there have been a tension between Christianity and the Roman Empire, considering that the religion of the Roman Empire was for the most part tolerant, open, and even hospitable in its relation to other religions?

Religion that is life-giving for all, according to the early Christians, proclaims the justice and righteousness of the God who embraces the foolishness, weakness, and resilience of the cross and the struggles of the people; malignant religion, on the other hand, embraces the logic of the wise and the powerful, which manifests itself in the oppression of the multitude (Jas 2:6-7) and the crucifixion of Jesus (1 Cor 1:18–2:8). There is a fundamental difference between the religion of privilege and its alternatives, and this is where Roman religious tolerance seems to have drawn a line. It was not by accident that Paul spent his ministry in and out of Roman prisons; neither should Jesus's death on a Roman cross come as a total surprise.

The life and ministry of Jesus embodies this tension between life-giving and malignant religion. Jesus, as we know him from the Gospels of the New Testament and a few historical records, takes a stand against the religion of the status quo embraced by many of his contemporaries. His controversies with certain powerful Pharisees and Sadducees (not all of them, to be sure) are well known—even to those who might not otherwise remember much else about him. His struggles with those whom the Gospel of John awkwardly and misleadingly calls "the Jews" are another example of the tension between different forms of religion, although easily misunderstood. At stake is not the struggle between Christianity and Judaism but the struggle between the dominant religion of the status quo and another religion embodied by Jesus and his followers, both located within the spectrum of the Jewish traditions.

At the heart of this tension between life-giving and malignant religion is the fundamental question of just who God is. Christians should never begin with the assumption that all who mention God, particularly when they call themselves Christian, are necessarily kindred spirits. Instead, when Christians reference God, a conversation begins: What God are we talking about? Just like there is a tension between life-giving and malignant religion, there is a tension between life-giving and malignant images of God and between life-giving and malignant images of Jesus Christ. Even some of our most cherished images of Jesus have been subject to the interpretive powers of empire.[5] Keep in mind also that what is life-giving and death-dealing may not always be immediately apparent.

> When Christians reference God, a conversation begins: What God are we talking about?

There are, of course, some clues and giveaways that we will develop throughout the book. In response to malignant religion, the voice of God proclaims in the book of Amos (5:24): "Let justice roll down like waters, and righteousness like an ever-flowing stream." In Isaiah, God presents this alternative to malignant religion: "Is not this the fast that I choose: to loose the bonds of injustice, to undo the thongs of the yoke, to let the oppressed go free, and to break every yoke? Is it not to share your bread with the hungry, and bring the homeless poor into your house; when you see the naked, to cover them, and not to hide yourself from your own kin?" (Isa 58:6-7).

Jesus, being deeply immersed in the live-giving traditions of Judaism, draws from these resources and picks them up in the Gospel of Luke: "The Spirit of the Lord is upon me, because he has anointed me to bring good news to the poor. He has sent me to proclaim release to the captives and recovery of sight to the blind, to let the oppressed go free, to proclaim the year of the Lord's favor" (4:18-19). It is not hard to see that this kind of religion is life-giving for all, not only for a small elite, and not only in the afterlife but especially here and now. Good news to the poor, for instance, is not only that they will go to heaven after they die but that they will no longer be poor here and now, that they will be able to feed their children, and that they will be able to live happy and productive lives that allow them to make positive contributions to their communities.

4

THE QUESTION WITH WHICH CHRISTIANITY STANDS OR FALLS

Today, this tension between life-giving and malignant religion—and particularly between life-giving and malignant Christianity—is once again the crucial issue. Failure to understand it has had disastrous consequences, both in the past and present. Here is a short list of some of the consequences that press us to search for alternatives:

1. Failure to understand this tension between live-giving and malignant religion has not only done damage to millions of people and the earth, it has also caused millions of people to abandon religion altogether. If God is identified with the dominant religion of the status quo, as is currently the case with most forms of Christian faith in the United States, millions more will abandon it as the malignant face of the status quo keeps revealing itself over and over again. Even today, some still have trouble seeing the corruptness of this status quo version of faith, but more and more are beginning to see it and turn away from Christianity or religion altogether.[6] And it's not only the younger generations that are sick and tired of toxic religion and its consequences (and those forms of faith that have lost the nerve to stand up to it). What forms of Christianity are maintaining the power to make a difference?

2. Failure to understand this tension between live-giving and malignant religion has allowed powerbrokers to mislead large numbers of well-meaning people. If religion is identified with a particular political program, as has often been the case in history, people who care about religion feel they have no choice but to accommodate. This is true even if the consequence might be the loss of human life or the destruction of life on the planet. The feeling that there is no alternative to the dominant Christianity of the powerbrokers has been destructive—even in the lives of people who care.

3. Failure to understand this tension between life-giving and malignant religion causes many to exchange their connectedness to the earth and its inhabitants for the proverbial pie in the sky of a heavenly reward. While this has gone on for centuries, the challenge to global survival is becoming more urgent every moment. Best-selling misinterpretations of the so-called rapture and apocalyptic end-time predictions, pie-in-the-sky theologies, and even liberal spiritual escapism have aggravated the situation and are likely leading us to the point of no return.

4. Failure to understand this tension between life-giving and malignant religion has seduced large numbers of people into blindly supporting economic systems that benefit elite minorities and relegate the vast majority of humanity and the planet to exploitation and suffering. While in the United States there is, at least on the books, the principle of the separation of church and state, there is no principle of the separation of church and economy. As a result, dominant religion and dominant economics reinforce each other so that Christianity has become one of the principal pillars of a particular form of capitalism promoted in the United States. What does it say that many Christians can imagine the end of the world but not the end of capitalism?

5. Failure to understand and engage this tension between life-giving and malignant religion has prevented not only life-giving Christianity from flourishing. It has also prevented life-giving inter-religious dialogue from taking off. Who would want to be in conversation with a religion that seeks to dominate the world, except those who also use their religious traditions for domination? While other religious traditions can also be implicated in domination, our concern with Jesus and Christianity in this book implies that we start with ourselves and rethink our cherished assumption that Christians have exclusive access to the "way, the truth, and the life" (John 14:6). What do these terms even mean?

The following chapters of this book correspond with these five challenges.

Chapter 1—Christians as Atheists? On the Heart of Christianity. The Roman leaders considered Christians to be atheists, not because they did not believe in a god but because their god did not fit the dominant definitions of a god. For the Romans, the attributes of a god had to match the attributes of the Roman Empire. A god who is understood in light of the life, death, and resurrection of Jesus Christ does not match these attributes and thus clashes with the expectations of empire. Here, Christianity (and perhaps religion itself) can be seen in a different light, and there is a choice to be made—not between faith and lack of faith, but between faith that is life-giving for all and faith that is not. Atheism—the rejection of the false god of dominant theism—is at the heart of this move.

Chapter 2—Give to Caesar What Is Caesar's and to God What Is God's: On Religion and Politics. What belongs to God? In a famous response to his opponents who challenge him about paying taxes to Caesar, Jesus implies that everything belongs to God. No political status quo can ever own religion, and any political approach must be subject to questioning, both from without and from within its circle of supporters. The politics of Jesus explored in this chapter can be taken seriously without confusing them with God and with religion, and no politician is ever "home free" without a consistent track record of support for what is life-giving for all. The politics of race will serve as a test case.

Chapter 3—The Materialism of Religion: On Religion and Things That Matter. Critics often point out that we have become too materialistic. By this they mean that we care too much about things and stuff. The remedy, it seems, is to become more spiritual. Jesus, taking a leaf from the Hebrew prophets, makes a different suggestion (Matt 11:4-5). He does not leave material reality to the powers of the Roman Empire but values it and transforms it for the benefit of the community. Both the material and the spiritual undergo a change here that produces new understandings of religion and of the world, contributing to the flourishing of all life.

Chapter 4—God vs. Mammon: On Religion and Economics. At the heart of Christianity is an understanding that a decision has to be made.

The key question that Jesus presents to his disciples and to Christians today is not whether we have faith or not, but in what do we believe and what holds our devotion (see, for example, Mark 8:27-29). What and whom should we trust in a world that demands trust above all in its basic economic structures, and what difference does it make? Here, we can start thinking about economics in alternative terms, informed by the economics of Jesus, and take some modest steps in directions that are geared toward sustaining life.

Chapter 5—The Way, the Truth, and the Life? On Interreligious and Other Dialogues. Dominant images of the truth are often unilateral. Empires are identified by their claim that there is no alternative. Jesus's claim to be the truth has a different flavor. It is the truth of the multitude that is more inclusive than is often recognized (John's "woman at the well"; Matthew's and Mark's "Syrophoenician woman"), yet it also has exclusive traits. Jesus's truth draws the line where empire rules with a deadly iron fist ("Who among you is the greatest?") and broadens the horizons when it comes to the least of these in the interest of supporting life. Samaritans and tax collectors who support the least of these are allies, religious officials who do not support the least of these are not. Here, interreligious dialogue takes off in directions that might be life-giving for all.

CONCLUSION

The tensions between Jesus and Caesar addressed in this book strike at the heart of Christianity. The tension is not about the personal relations of two individuals (Jesus never met Augustus or Tiberius—the Roman emperors of his time); the tension is between two ways of life that include religion, culture, politics, economics, and everything else that makes us human.

When we talk about Jesus, to be sure, we are talking about a specific individual, but we know him through the communities that have kept and are keeping his witness alive. When we talk about Caesar, we can also refer to specific individuals—Gaius Julius Caesar was the name of the first Roman emperor, after Rome moved from being a republic to being an empire—but for the most part we are using the name as a title. *Caesar* (morphed into the German *Kaiser*) came to mean emperor. And while the emperors of Rome were distinct individuals, for everyday life in the Roman Empire, especially in faraway places like Galilee and Palestine, change of individuals at the top would not have always been noticeable.

Of course, if Caesar is the embodiment of dominant power and dominant religion, why should he even be concerned about Jesus? Why bother with the Jesus movement, which was probably rather small in numbers, and why bother with emerging Christianity, which initially was a minute minority in the Roman Empire? The same questions might be raised today, when status quo Christianity dominates and attracts most of the attention, while life-giving Christianity often finds itself in the minority and is ignored.

The answer has to do with the simple fact that the Jesus movement made a difference and that Christianity continues to make a difference, in however limited a form. Keep in mind that imperial and colonial systems are never totally accepted and that resilience and resistance can never be completely repressed. At times even silence can be a powerful expression of pushback.[7] Moreover, in order to make a difference it is not necessary to resolve all problems or to claim perfection—empires are often challenged by alternative ways of life that they cannot control and challenged by ambivalence.[8]

Thus, even relatively small movements have sometimes brought change—experts talk about a critical mass of only 3 percent of the population! Those in power sense this and fight back, from the persecution of the early Christians to US government-led efforts to eliminate Latin American liberation theology and many other attempts to silence alternative Christianity.[9] The experience of imperial pushback can be one sign that we are doing something right.

> The tension is between two ways of life that include religion, politics, economics, and everything else that makes us human....Empires are often challenged by alternative ways of life that they cannot control.

But how can we know and embody the difference of Jesus if the imagination of Caesar has shaped us to the core, often shaping our images of Jesus as well? In this book, we draw on core traditions that we encounter in the Gospels, in the context of the emerging faith of the church and on the background of the ancient Jewish traditions that shaped Jesus and the early Christians.[10] We are holding together what has often been separated, history and faith (the historical Jesus and the Christ of dogma shape each other), humanity and divinity (what is human and divine cannot be separated in Jesus but each influences the other), and public and private (religion, politics, and economics cannot be divided in Jesus's life). In the spirit of the ancient Council of Chalcedon (451 CE), there is no need to separate these categories, but there is also no need to confuse them.[11]

The images of Jesus that emerge in this book are, thus, informed both by historical and theological scholarship with a keen eye on the struggles of the present. Understanding Jesus in his historical and theological context matters, but only if it is developed in light of our own historical and theological context.[12] Historical and theological critiques are, thus, becoming historical and theological self-critiques, geared to help us discern the difference between Jesus and Caesar both then and now. In this context, the contemporary struggles for life and death help us see the struggles of the past more clearly, and vice versa. More specifically, those who are forced to endure the greatest pressures in this struggle in their own bodies are the ones who can help us see both Jesus and ourselves more clearly, and they throw fresh light on Caesar as well.[13] Due to my own engagement in liberation movements that spans several decades, these perspectives are always part of my reflections, even if they are not named explicitly. To be sure: liberation movements themselves are in constant need of self-critical reflection.[14]

In this work, we are in conversation with resources drawn from the Gospels but also from the witness of Paul, whose images of Christ frequently turn out to be anti-imperial, and the broad and deep Jewish traditions, from which both Jesus and Paul drew. In particular, we will engage the spirit of the Lord's prayer according to the Gospel of Matthew (6:9-13), which constitutes a revolutionary manifesto of sorts:

Our Father in heaven,
   hallowed be your name.
Your kingdom come.
  Your will be done,
    on earth as it is in heaven.
Give us this day our daily bread.
And forgive us our debts,
   as we also have forgiven our debtors.
And do not bring us to the time of trial
   but rescue us from the evil one.

It is our hope that when churches become aware of the difference Jesus and his movement made in the tensions of the world of the Roman Empire, they can more fully follow Jesus and make a difference in the tensions of the world today. Like the Jesus movement, this will not put them in a position to control the world, but many people would receive them with open arms and—who knows?—good news rather than bad news might eventually be brought to the poor and to the rest of creation.

QUESTIONS FOR REFLECTION AND DISCUSSION

1. What is the fundamental tension between Jesus and Caesar, and why is religion part of the problem?

2. How does the tension between Jesus and Caesar manifest itself within Christianity today?

3. Where do you see your own faith community making positive differences?

Chapter 1
CHRISTIANS AS ATHEISTS?

On the Heart of Christianity

Failure to understand the tension between life-giving and malignant religion (and choose between them) has not only done damage to millions of people and to the earth, but it has also caused millions more to abandon religion altogether. If God is identified with the dominant religion of the status quo, it may appear to those who see the faith-buttressed powers oppressing, exploiting, and excluding others that we have only two options: continue to hold on to this version of God, hoping that a little reform might bring things back into alignment—or sever their allegiance to God altogether.

Sometimes the second option is projected onto those who seek to follow an undomesticated Jesus. A recent response to the Moral Mondays movement serves as one example of the current clash between conservative and progressive versions of Christian faith. Many appreciate Rev. William Barber's efforts to reclaim Christian values in a world that shows little concern for the least of these, yet Barber has been charged with atheism by some, including the Reverend Franklin Graham.[1] This sort of accusation against progressive Christianity from conservative religious camps is not uncommon. But is Graham right? Is this a fair assessment of Barber's faith? He is right that Barber rejects the god of dominant Christianity's status quo, but Graham's charge of atheism fails to understand that some forms of atheism do not result in the rejection of God altogether. In fact, some kinds of atheism turn out to be necessary components in the search for the true God, at the heart of Christianity.

> Some kinds of atheism turn out to be necessary components in the search for the true God, at the heart of Christianity.

While atheism can mean the rejection of any god, the term is better understood as the rejection of particular theisms, that is, particular understandings of God. Rejecting the theism of the status quo, for instance, can mean rejecting images of a god who supports the wealthy and condemns the poor; who sanctions whatever power rules supreme at the moment in politics, economics, and religion; and who shows little concern or compassion for the least of these. Rejecting such images of God means to take a stand against certain forms of theism, but it need not mean rejecting God altogether. This nuanced understanding of atheism reflects the fundamental struggle at the heart of Christianity between false gods and the true God.[2]

> A nuanced understanding of atheism reflects the fundamental struggle at the heart of Christianity between false gods and the true God.

Surprisingly, the charge of atheism places contemporary Christians in the esteemed company of early Christians in the Roman Empire, who were charged in similar fashion. Like the Reverend Graham accused the Reverend Barber, Roman philosophers accused Christians of atheism. They, too, had a point, as these Christians did in fact reject images of God modeled after the image of Caesar and the ruling elites. Because they rejected images of God that were considered traditional and conservative (in the sense that they conserved the definitions, practices, and power relationships of the status quo), early Christians were declared atheists.

14

Since these Christians knew what they were doing, they probably took the charge of atheism as a compliment (a false god is no god at all).

Interesting in both cases is not merely what divine images are rejected but what fresh images of God are emerging. Might there be parallels between images of God in early Christianity and in forms of Christianity today that refuse to align with the status quo, and what might those look like? How did Jesus influence the way Christians envision God (then and now), and how is this different from the religion of Caesar, whose traditionalism conserves and maintains a social and political state of affairs?

How we see God active in the world matters. Much is at stake in how we answer these questions, because our images of God affect a range of things, from the survival of whom Jesus calls "the least of these" to the flourishing of the planet and the future of Christianity. How we see God working in the world matters. And seeking answers is not merely the task of a few theologians or Christians who want to know more about their faith. More and more North Americans, especially young adults, are worried about the increasingly hostile and destructive nature of a Christianity that simply goes with the dominant culture's flow, oblivious and even callous in the face of others' suffering. Many are equally worried about a church that has lost the nerve to stand up to what they consider blatant abuses of the name of God by a religion that espouses racism, sexism, homophobia, and that seems indifferent or unconcerned about ever-growing inequality. Do we have to envision God in terms of the rules of dominant theism, as an elitist dictator, a heavenly bully, or a supernatural control freak?[3]

People who want to take their faith seriously face a conundrum: Do they follow self-proclaimed conservatives (like Franklin Graham and others) who set themselves up as the keepers of Christian tradition even when they appear to be following Caesar rather than Jesus? Must they align themselves with some prominent atheists like Christopher Hitchens or Richard Dawkins who point out the fundamental inconsistencies of this faith and its destructive nature, abandoning their faith and church itself as beyond rescue?

15

Or could they reclaim a faith that is energized by drawing on how Jesus actually embodies images of God that contrast with those of the empires of their times, even if it means being charged with atheism, treason, or worse?

THE CONFLICT OF ATHEISM: NOT WHAT WE THOUGHT

Roman philosophers considered Christians to be atheists, not because they didn't believe in God, but because their God did not fit the dominant definitions of divinity backed by time-honored traditions. For the Romans, the attributes of a god had to match imperial attributes, as did the deities that were assembled in their pantheon. Extended to the doctrines that are shared by most adherents of classical philosophical theism, God had to be omnipotent, omniscient, omnipresent, immutable, and impassible.[4]

The claim of being all-powerful illustrates what is at stake: declaring that all power is in the hands of God in terms of omnipotence also means declaring that God is not subject to any other power. As a result, many traditional theists would also have to believe that such a God must be impassible—unmoved by the world's pain—because God would cease to be all-powerful if anything could touch God, affect God, or make God suffer. Theology and the politics of empire are in alignment here: God's power is seen through the lens of empire, a structure considered strongest when ruled by one person at the top who controls everything and in whom all power is concentrated.

It is not hard to see that a God who is understood in light of the life, death, and resurrection of Jesus Christ contradicts most of these attributes. This was not lost on the Romans, and so they charged Christians who worshiped a crucified God with atheism. Even though there were plenty of efforts to defend Christians against this charge by early Christian theologians like Justin Martyr and Athenagoras,[5] the Roman charge of atheism has a point: the God of Jesus Christ does not match dominant

16

cultural ideas of divinity. This crucial difference is sometimes lost when telling the history of Christianity, making Christian faith look like any other empire religion and confusing Christians: if God's relationship to us is from the top down and one-way only, as it is with the classical definition of omnipotence, God can't listen. What sense would it make to pray to such a god?

So maybe the charge of atheism is good news rather than bad news. Wouldn't it be good news to many contemporaries who have grown sick of the past two thousand years of worshiping the unreceptive and self-centered gods of successive empires? While the early Christian apologists sought to show that Christianity was no threat to the Roman Empire,[6] what if it really did present a threat? This threat takes shape in two diametrically opposed logical structures and value-worlds. According to one logic, the power of God resembles the power of the empire, "power over," operating from the top down, affected by no one; according to the other logic, the power of God takes a shape that moves in a different direction, embodying and actively seeking relationship with struggling humanity and all of creation.

For early Christians the tension between conservative Roman theism and their belief in God was rooted in their understanding of Jesus Christ, the person for whom they were nicknamed. According to the testimonies of these early Christians recorded in the New Testament, Jesus's whole way of life (not merely his theology and his ideas) contested top-down power. And if that was not enough to challenge status quo theism, Jesus was anything but impassible. He was moved by the pain and suffering of others and he lived a passionate life. His constant run-ins with the authorities, from local synagogue leaders all the way up to the high priests—often protégées of the Roman rulers—speak volumes on the matter. His stunt of mimicking the powerful entry of the Roman governor on horseback into Jerusalem by riding on a donkey (Mark 11:1-11)—while an act of humility—was also a blatant challenge of top-down power that would not have been lost on both his followers and the broader public. His untimely death on a cross was another unmistakable indication of an open conflict with the imperial powers, because this is how insurgents under Roman rule were dealt with to deter further insurgencies.[7]

That Jesus showed not only compassion but also raw passion is well known even by people who have only cursory knowledge of the Bible, though some of us who have spent our lives in churches often seem to forget this. In the Gospels Jesus weeps over the fate of Jerusalem (Luke 19:41), gets acutely angry and goes on the attack in the holy place of the temple in Jerusalem where most people would consider it least appropriate (Luke 19:45-46), extends both love and tough love (Luke 19:41-44; 20:45-47), and even gets severely depressed: "I am deeply grieved, even to death" (Mark 14:34). Neither could it be claimed that Jesus is immutable (unmoved or unchanged by the world around him); on occasions he even appears to change his mind, like in the conversation with the Syrophoenician woman whose daughter he heals, despite first refusing to do so (Mark 7:24-30).

The Apostle Paul notes the scandalous nature of talking about a Jesus who constantly gets in trouble and ends up on the cross (for reasons that make sense to the status quo). Paul, who turns out not to be quite the conformist that the church imagines him to be, claims that the "Christ crucified" is "a stumbling block to Jews and foolishness to Gentiles" (1 Cor 1:23). To those who get it, however, he notes (other Jews and Gentiles included) "Christ is the power of God and the wisdom of God. For God's foolishness is wiser than human wisdom and God's weakness is stronger than human strength" (1 Cor 1:24-25). To be sure, this is not a rejection of the Jewish religion or of Gentiles in general; the point is that proclaiming the resilient power of God's weakness was—and still is—a challenge to the dominant powers that model themselves after omnipotence. The same is true for proclaiming the foolishness of God in the face of dominant wisdom.

> Proclaiming the resilient power of God's weakness was—and still is—a challenge to the dominant powers that model themselves after omnipotence.

18

Tensions with the powers that be—whether they are political, economic, or religious—are, thus, to be expected. The faith of these early Christians was not merely of a different kind but it clashed with the dominant faiths of the Roman Empire. Why would the existence of tensions surprise us today? Rather than signifying the absence of faith, in fact, tension with power may be the sign of a truly vibrant faith. Unfortunately, many communities of faith today shy away from any conflict and, as a result, faith that conforms to the traditions of empire usually wins the day. Without opposition, the dominant position prevails.

In sum, early Christians were not merely considered atheists by default or by accident. Following Jesus, their message, their faith, and their way of life actively provoked this classification. As a result, the tradition of Christians being considered atheists in the Roman Empire is a source of pride—something to be cherished—not something to be ashamed of. Today, why not reclaim those traditions in the face of another dominant theism that claims the mantle of conserving the tradition? Which traditions will we follow? Those that proclaim that God is on the side of the powerful, the strong, the successful, and the wealthy? Those that claim God blesses America no matter what it does and that some "others" are less valuable because of the their skin color, gender, sexual orientation, or economic status?

Now, as then, rejecting the traditions of Caesarian theism and embracing the traditions of Jesus marks the heart of a life-giving Christianity, helping us avoid our deep-seated predisposition to serve the wrong God.

WRONG GOD: WHAT DIFFERENCE DOES IT MAKE?

While there is no full-fledged doctrine of the Trinity in the New Testament, the early Christians believed that Jesus was more than a role model or a powerful prophet. They expressed this faith by praying to him. What made Jesus so scandalous for the religion of Caesar had to do not only with his unconventional ways of life but also with his close relationship to God.

Unlike in the Jewish faith, in the Roman religious imagination it was not scandalous to elevate a human being to the ranks of the gods. Several of the Roman emperors were considered divine or claimed divinity for themselves. While humans could thus be divine, what was scandalous for the Romans was to claim divinity for this particular person. As John Dominic Crossan puts it, "it is not absurd...to claim that Jesus was *divine*, but it is absurd to claim that *Jesus* was divine."[8]

Jesus embodied the opposite of everything that characterized divinity in the Roman Empire: death on a cross (as the conclusion of a life lived in solidarity with regular working people), birth into a family of day laborers in construction, head-on challenges to dominant interpretations of rules and laws and sometimes the rules themselves, and resistance to dominant authorities such as the temple in Jerusalem (that bore some of the insignia of the Roman Empire, including its eagle). How could this particular individual be considered God?

The titles of Jesus in early Christianity further illustrate this clash. Today, we tend to assume that titles like *savior* or even *lord* are of purely religious origin. In the first centuries, however, these titles were political and economic as well, given to the Roman emperor. Caesar was "lord and savior," and claiming these titles for anyone else would have amounted to treason. Keep in mind that there was no separation of politics, economics, and religion at that time, so that it would not have been an option to hold that Caesar was the political lord and savior and Jesus was the religious one. This Jesus could not be relegated to the realm of harmless personal piety and religiosity—a persistent challenge in our time, when many Christians think that they can consign Jesus to their private lives and the inside of church buildings.

Why would early Christians have selected titles like savior and lord for Jesus when these were also the titles of the Roman emperors? Other titles would have readily been available, taken from the so-called mystery cults or from the Jewish traditions, like master, redeemer, or messiah. Many biblical scholars agree that early Christians like Paul used these titles intentionally in order to juxtapose the reality of Jesus Christ with the presumptive and posturing reality of the Roman emperors:[9] the power of Jesus was and is fundamentally different from the power of emperors. Jesus the lord and savior was fundamentally different from the Roman emperor as lord and savior—and from any other power broker since. Jesus did not embody top-down power but bottom-up power. He embraced the power of resilience embodied in the movements of common people, then and now.

> Jesus did not embody top-down power but bottom-up power. He embraced the power of resilience that is embodied in the movements of common people, then as now.

This alternative power can be seen in Jesus's ministry in Galilee and Judea, where his work helped organize and revitalize depressed village communities that had come under pressure by the Roman Empire and its local representatives like Herod and his sons. Calling the people blessed (blessed are the poor) and challenging their oppressors (and woe to you rich) was revolutionary and a game-changer that turned things upside down (see Luke 6). No longer can the poor be blamed for their misfortune—a lesson that continues to be relevant to this day![10] No wonder Caesar was not pleased.

Paul's ministry in the eastern part of the wider Roman Empire embodied alternative power as well, embracing God's election of the weak over and against the strong, the foolish over and against the wise, and those who are somebodies over and against those who are nobodies (1 Cor. 1:26-29). And Paul in his own way experienced this resilient power in weakness (2 Cor 12:9).

And while the emperor was considered the savior—the one who promised to provide for the welfare of his people in both spiritual and material ways—Jesus the savior provided spiritual and material welfare as well. The difference being that the salvation Jesus offered was intended not

21

to neglect the welfare of the "least of these" but to begin with them and make them the benchmark and measure of his ministry (Matt 25:31-46). Here, for the writer of Matthew's Gospel, the judgment depends on how whole communities (the "nations") relate or fail to relate to those who are hungry, thirsty, strangers, naked, sick, and in prison. If these were our criteria for saving provision—and indeed for salvation itself—how would Christian communities in the United States fare?

> The salvation Jesus offered was intended not to neglect the welfare of the "least of these" but to begin with them and make them the benchmark and measure of his ministry (Matt 25:31-46).

If these were merely private religious commitments held by pious individuals, it is likely that none of them would have caused anyone to worry. After all, the Roman Empire was not particularly threatened by what happened behind the closed doors of the mystery cults of the time. Neither did the empire have a problem with religious plurality, managing to incorporate a few other divine figures into its pantheon as long as they didn't rock the boat. So why was Christianity different? Why did it represent such a challenge to the Roman Empire?

Adopting prominent terms like *lord* and *savior* points to courageous efforts not only to challenge the authority and power of the empire but also to provide significant and viable alternatives to it. To be sure, these efforts did not take shape in grandiose forms, since Christian communities were still small. But the alternatives were real, expressed in concrete faith communities who found power and welfare not with the emperor but in their own faithful efforts: sharing things in common (Acts 2 and 4), worshiping a non-tyrannical force at work among the common people (Mark 4:30-32), and forming different kinds of relationships that undermined dominant portraits of status and strength.

The resulting pushback that early Christianity received from the Roman Empire, replete with persecutions and executions, shows that it must have hit a nerve and that it was perhaps more powerful than anyone gave it credit. Today, a closer look at when and where pushback against this resilient power occurs may offer answers and point us in the direction of the God we encounter in Jesus Christ.[11]

WRONG GOD, RIGHT GOD: THE STRUGGLE CONTINUES

As Pope Francis recently suggested, it is better to be an atheist than a bad Christian.[12] However, "bad Christians"—to whom the pope directed this challenge—are not just those who are hypocrites. Bad Christians are also those who fervently want to be good Christians—those who mean well, but are misguided. This is, arguably, the deeper problem of our time, one that doesn't make it any easier to deal with questions of allegiance to the God of Jesus and malignant forms of faith.

The religion of the empire can be deceptive because it usually presents itself as a good and positive thing, concerned about the salvation and the welfare of the people. Even the most self-serving empires, then as now, claim that their goal is to make people happy and to bring peace. For two thousand years, many Christians and churches have fallen for this, even as in many cases the narcissism of empire and the severity of its inequalities have grown worse. Keep in mind that in the Roman Empire of 150 CE the top 1 percent controlled merely 16 percent of all wealth, while in the United States today the top 1 percent control more than 40 percent of all wealth.[13] If Caesar and the Roman Empire give us pause, should we not be even more concerned today? Since the religion of the empire claims to be conserving time-honored traditions, which traditions are we talking about?

The story of struggle between Jesus and Caesar continues in the fourth century CE, when the emperor Constantine—the Caesar of his time—set the stage for what became one of the greatest compromises of Christianity in history. As we consider Constantine, keep in mind that contemporary accommodations of Christian faith to the surrounding culture resemble what happened then, with a few twists: today, these concessions are less conscious because most of us assume the separation of church and state, and we often justify our compromises since they are now part of the tradition.

Because Constantine thought he experienced the support of the Christian God in his military victory over his rival Licinius, he embraced Christianity and thus elevated its place in the Roman Empire. To be sure, Constantine's idea of the Christian God resembles the top-down God embodied by a dominant form of classical theism, and it is this image of God that continues to shape Christianity. In 325 CE, Constantine calls (and funds) the Council of Nicaea, bringing together Christian bishops from around the empire. He also presides over the council and, as the story goes, suggests the central theological term of the resulting Nicene Creed, *homoousios*. This Greek term said that Jesus was of the same substance as God (hence, *homo*—same, *ousia*—being or substance). It was designed to settle the debate between Christians who believed Jesus to be fully God and the so-called Arians who believed that Jesus, while very special and important, was not fully God.[14]

While the Nicene Creed has become a staple for many church traditions and is still in use today, there are a least two very different ways to interpret it, resulting in two distinct traditions with quite different images of God, and mirroring the ongoing conflict between Jesus and Caesar. The more common interpretation follows what Constantine would most likely have had in mind, declaring that Jesus is fully God in terms of the ideas of classical imperial theism, omnipotent and impassible. This God operates from the top down, just like the emperor, as both are seen as the pinnacle of dominant power and imagined as mostly unaffected by interests other than their own.

In this reading, the declaration that "Jesus is like God" remakes our image of Jesus in terms of the god of the empire and the emperor himself.[15] Here, there is no longer a conflict between Jesus and Caesar, as Jesus has become Caesar. In artists' renderings of the period, Jesus appears as a ruler dressed in royal robes rather than as an itinerant preacher or shepherd. In this way, Jesus is assimilated into the value world of empire, endorsing and shoring it up. Professing Jesus as Lord now no longer contradicts the lordship of the emperor—or of anyone else holding great and unilateral power (like some present-day CEOs), but rather endorses it.

There is, however, another way to interpret the Nicene Creed that poses a stark challenge to empire. This challenge might offer one explanation for why Constantine later in life abandoned aspects of the Nicene Creed and was baptized by an Arian bishop on his deathbed. If Jesus shares the same nature as God, as the creed says, why not turn things around and interpret the nature of God in terms of Jesus's life and work rather than interpreting Jesus in terms of the empire-god? In this case, God's power is understood not in terms of empire-like omnipotence but in terms of how Jesus wielded power, namely in resilient service and in deep solidarity.[16] In this case, there is now a radical edge to the doctrine of the Trinity. Not only is Jesus diametrically opposed to Caesar, but God is too.[17]

> If Jesus is of the same nature as God, as the creed says, why not turn things around and interpret the nature of God in terms of Jesus's life and work? In this case, God's power is understood not in terms of empire-like omnipotence but in terms of how Jesus wielded power, namely in resilient service and in deep solidarity.

The Gospel episode where Jesus tells John and James that "whoever wishes to be great among you must be your servant . . . for the Son of Man came not to be served but to serve" is well known (Mark 10:43, 45). Instead of accommodation to the tradition of empire, the Jesus tradition provides alternatives to imperial rule. And these alternatives—something we explore throughout this book—liberate us from the tiresome service of the wrong god who refuses to serve.

Moreover, as other ancient theologians would have intuitively known, the unilateral rule of the empire is weakened if there are two emperors at the top instead of just one.[18] This concern, rather than liberal theological sentiments, may have been the reason why the Arians were worried about declaring Jesus to be fully divine and why Constantine at the end of his life reverted to Arianism. The matter only got more complex when the Holy Spirit was added to the doctrine of the Trinity as a third person, equal to the other two. But perhaps this is part of the genius of the Christianity that finds its inspiration in Jesus: power does not have to be directed unilaterally from the top; power can be shared among equals who embody unity in difference, like the three persons of the Trinity. Those who assume that Trinitarian theology is the exclusive domain of the traditions of self-proclaimed conservative Christianity may want to think again.

Alternative images of God are, of course, not entirely new and unique to Jesus; they are firmly rooted in ancient traditions. The Jewish traditions contain images of a God who sides with the people against empires, whether in Ancient Egypt or Babylonia. This God refuses to endorse kings because their rule exploits people (1 Sam 8:1-18). This God works through service and solidarity with the people, whether during the exodus from Egypt or the Babylonian Exile. Throughout the ages, such alternative images never disappeared completely, breaking through in various periods, including today, in different kinds of liberative theologies grounded in communities struggling to be free. The history and theology of African American slaves in the United States, who envisioned God as their sustainer and liberator, is only one example.

Ultimately, these alternative traditions resonate with and make a lot more sense to many contemporary readers and those who are beginning to doubt positions of top-down control and unilateral power. Why should African Americans believe that God identifies with white America, why should immigrants believe that God cares less about them than about their hosts, or why should working people believe that God is found primarily on the side of their bosses? Or, for that matter, why should even the bosses believe in themselves if their track record is less than perfect?

The tradition of Caesar promised happiness and peace if people worshiped and served him; today, neoliberal capitalism is promising the same things once again.[19] Yet these promises have hardly been fulfilled for the majority of the population. Suffering and pain experienced by so many are bound to raise questions. In the words of Frederick Herzog: "You don't understand what theology is unless you have looked in the face of suffering, unless you have become an atheist in the presence of pain."[20] In addition to widespread global misery, seeing 21 percent of children at home living below the poverty level and 43 percent in low-income families, with poverty rates even higher in black, Latino, and Native American children,[21] raises not only questions about how the dominant system is performing, it also raises deep theological questions about whether the God we are serving is the right one. The god of Caesar is not compatible with the God of Jesus.

Perhaps the Jewish philosopher Ernst Bloch was right when he argued that only an atheist can be a good Christian and, vice versa, only a Christian can be a good atheist.[22] While this argument should not be limited to Christianity, it captures something of the particular character of Christianity, which has its origins in the incompatibility of Jesus vs. Caesar.

RIGHT GOD: "HALLOWED BE YOUR NAME"

The struggle between true and false gods is firmly rooted in the Jewish traditions. The first two of the Ten Commandments prohibit having other gods ("you shall have no other gods," [Exod 20:3]), making idols, and "bow[ing] down to them and worship[ing] them" (Exod 20:4-5). At stake is not merely belief in other gods but the worshiping and the serving of them. The problem with the theism of the status quo, therefore, is not merely a matter of belief or of the intellect but of a way of life that includes worshiping and serving the wrong gods to the detriment of the well-being of other people and the environment.

The alternative, entering into a relationship with the God of Israel and of Jesus, is likewise not merely a matter of belief or intellect but has to do with alternative ways of life and alternative ways of worshiping and serving. These ways of life have the potential to be life-giving, as they are linked up with mutually beneficial relations to others and to the environment—the point of the remaining eight commandments.

27

The beginning of the Lord's Prayer (Matt 6:9) picks up the Ten Commandments' concern with worship and service of the right God, as it addresses God directly: "Hallowed be your name." More than just a pious phrase, this statement points to the heart of Christianity. If having other gods and making idols of things that are not god leads to misguided service, hallowing the name of God might lead to more appropriate service. This is the point of the following petitions of the Lord's Prayer, like the breaking in of the reign of God here and now (kingdom), having enough food (bread), mutual forgiveness of debt, and deliverance from evil. Each of these petitions will be picked up in one of the following chapters.

In the context of the Roman Empire, worshiping and serving the God of Jesus Christ meant a way of life that conflicted with the reign of Caesar—a reign that made the powerful more powerful and the weak weaker, the rich richer and the poor poorer. The way of life informed by the reign of God embodied in the life of Jesus was diametrically opposed to the reign of Caesar, ushering in the liberation of the oppressed and good news to the poor (Matt 11:5; Luke 4:18). To be sure, good news to the poor, as we shall see in the next chapters, cannot be limited to going to heaven after death or to being dependent on someone else's charity. If good news to the poor does not refer to the end of the conditions that keep creating and re-creating poverty, can it be good news?

Today, hallowing God's name means not assuming that when politicians or pastors talk about God they are necessarily talking about the God of Jesus Christ. Since the tradition of the god of Caesar is often still the dominant one today, Christians need to ask questions about God in order to make sure their worship and service is directed toward the right God. Referencing tradition and God is not the end of the debate—referencing tradition and God is the beginning of a critical conversation where each side needs to provide compelling, gospel-rooted arguments. God's name is hallowed when easy God-talk gives way to more thoughtful conversations.

In this context, even time-honored theological questions that might have been considered settled appear in new light. The Protestant tradition on justification by grace through faith (Eph 2:8) may serve as an example. In Paul's theology, the notion of justification was developed in contrast to the theology of the Roman Empire.[23] What images of the divine are at work here? Even if the Roman goddess Justitia was blindfolded to symbolize neutrality, the justice of empires often favors their most prominent clients, those with power, money, privilege, and accomplishment who have the right kinds of connections, who can afford the best lawyers, and who thus seemingly need neither grace nor faith.

At the time of Nero, the Roman writer Petronius wrote this poem:

Of what avail are laws
where money rules alone
and the poor suitor
can never succeed?
So a lawsuit
is nothing but a public auction,
and the knightly juror who listens to the case
gives his vote as he is PAID.[24]

Our contemporary situation reflects a similar dynamic, as a supposedly neutral justice system still tends to favor those with power, influence, and money. White-collar crime, for instance, is often judged less harshly than other crimes, both by the justice system and in public opinion. And while more white people use illegal drugs than black people, to give another example, more black people end up in prison. More minorities are caught up in the prison-industrial complex and more of them are likely to be put to death.[25]

The traditional concern of the Protestant Reformers of the sixteenth century about "works-righteousness" also appears in different light here. Works-righteousness, the effort to earn divine justification by doing good works, is not a problem of humanity in general (as is often assumed) but a trait of the elites who act as if they have special access to God and who tend to assume that they can manipulate God. Such works-righteousness is one of the core problems of empires and their false gods, at work in the times of both Paul and the Reformers, and even today. Things only change when the dominant notion of justification by works is rejected and replaced with justification by grace. Justification by grace means that the true God, whose name Christians seek to hallow, is not the one who caters to the interests of the elites but the one who cares about those who know that they cannot save themselves—the majority of humanity, like ordinary working people, slaves, women, and many others who do not belong to the ranks of the elite.

Unlike the justice of Caesar, the justice that Jesus represents is not biased toward the powerful and the rich, nor is this justice merely neutral. The justice for which Jesus stands means that God is taking the side of those who are in need of grace in situations of pressure and need, the ones who have no illusions about their ability to pull themselves up by their own bootstraps. This is also the notion of justice that is at work throughout the Hebrew Bible, from the exodus to the prophets. Jesus and Paul are in agreement on this point.[26]

> The justice for which Jesus stands means that God is taking the side of those who are in need of grace in situations of pressure and need, the ones who have no illusions about their ability to pull themselves up by their own bootstraps.

How did this understanding of Jesus in contrast to Caesar manifest itself later on in the Roman Empire, when Constantine officially recognized and promoted Christianity? For Constantine, Christianity was of value as a force that unified the empire and promoted its values. A reading of the Nicene Creed that identified Jesus with a god of the empire was an important step in this direction. Here, however, one of the major problems of worshiping and serving the wrong god comes to the surface: while such worship and service may unify a community or even a nation, it does so in terms of the interest of the dominant minority instead of the majority, in terms of the interests of the powerful instead of the interests of the people.

Jesus also restores community, but in very different ways. As recent New Testament scholarship has pointed out, one of the most important concerns of Jesus was to restore the covenant community of the people of

30

Israel in the face of the fragmentation that was produced by experiences of exploitation and oppression.[27] In the Gospels, Jesus restores community not by creating unity in terms of a top-down power; to the contrary, Jesus restores community by challenging the dominant forces of elitist religion and other structures (who are my mother and my sisters and brothers? [Mark 3:31-35]) in order to bring people together on different terms. And the community is made up of those who serve the true God (Mark 3:35: "Whoever does the will of God is my brother and sister and mother").

In today's context experiences of fragmentation are—like in Jesus's time—common: between those of different races, ethnic and gender identities, and diverse social, economic, and political allegiances. Once again, the empire has found ways to unify people by promoting the traditions of wrong gods, in particular the god of nationalism but also the god of consumption. Rather than unifying people in terms of slavish commitment to the traditions of empire, however, serving the traditions of the right God might help us to create a very different kind of community beginning with the interests of the "least of these" (Matt 25:31-46). Only if they flourish can all of us flourish.

CONCLUSION: FAITH BETWEEN LIFE AND DEATH

Being called atheists in the battle against the traditions of Caesar and the gods of the reigning status quo appears to put Christians at a disadvantage. When the Roman elites talked about God, they had in mind the god of the embodied imperial power. Something similar appears to be true today. When people talk about God, they have in mind the traditions of a dominant ruling force that is somehow linked with people who have power and that endorses the way things are at the moment. Sometimes this is explicitly called a "higher power" or couched in the language of "God and country."

Can this battle between the traditions of Jesus and Caesar be won by anyone else but Caesar? When the question is framed this way, an interesting reversal occurs. While the Roman emperors did in fact win many decisive battles and ruled over vast populations and territories, they never were able to subjugate all alternative ways of life, and in the end the Roman Empire itself broke apart and collapsed. History shows that this has been the fate of every empire on the planet, and there is no reason to assume that current regimes and their Caesars will fare any better. While the followers of Jesus have little reason to brag—alternative Christianity has often been small and sometimes messy—they are the ones who have on occasion been able to embody counter-imperial ways of life that keep presenting challenges to the status quo, the kind that in the long arc of history sometimes prevail. They are the ones who have taken up the cause of the least of these with some success. And across time, slaves are freed and the poor receive good news.

Here, Christianity (and perhaps religion itself) can be seen in a different light, not as an appendage to the powers that be but as providing real-life alternatives, however small and inadequate they may seem to be. Observing the traditions of Jesus teaches us that religion does not have to adorn the status quo; religion can also be that which makes a difference and provides another way of life. This religion is not a matter of embracing some generic faith that is part of the dominant system and then going with the flow—just the opposite: this religion calls us to make a choice, not between faith and lack of faith but between faith traditions that are life-giving and those that are not.

QUESTIONS FOR REFLECTION AND DISCUSSION

1. What questionable images of God do you encounter in your own communities?

2. How might atheism, as the rejection of misguided theisms, help us develop more appropriate images of God?

3. How might images of Jesus help us set the theological record straight in the context of severe distortions?

Chapter 2
GIVE TO CAESAR WHAT IS CAESAR'S AND TO GOD WHAT IS GOD'S

On Religion and Politics

Failure to understand the tension between life-giving and malignant religion leads to what may be the most significant challenge facing those who seek to truly follow Jesus today. When all religion is assumed to be the same we're faced with two options: one is to reject religion altogether, and the other is to go along with whatever the current dominant form of Christian faith demands. This false choice has permitted the defenders of the status quo, and in particular certain politicians, to mislead large numbers of well-meaning people who are committed to their faith. This false choice throws some light on current voting patterns, too. Isn't it odd that Christians often vote for political candidates who claim religion, even though they have surprisingly little in common with the Jesus whom Christians seek to follow?

If religion is identified with a particular established political party, as has often been the case historically and has become increasingly common in the United States,[1] the faithful are made to feel as if they have no choice but to comply. This is strangely the case even when the consequence is loss of human lives or the destruction of life on the planet. The widespread

33

impression that there is no faithful alternative to dominant forms of Christianity is destroying not only those who are thrown under the bus of this form of religion but—to some degree—even its reluctant adherents who feel that they have no choice but to continue with business as usual.

Empire wants us to believe that there is no alternative—the Roman Empire under Caesar is just one example. This is what Jesus was up against, and this is what we are up against today, with the ironic twist that images of Jesus have been more and more pulled into the schemes of empire.[2] In this chapter we will argue that the opposite is true, namely that there are always alternatives, not just in people's minds but in real life. Such alternatives are found, for example, in the politics of Jesus explored in this chapter and its contribution to ongoing change in the world for two millennia. Jesus embodies a kind of politics that is judged not by great ideas, party lines, or by meaning well. And for the Jesus of the New Testament, this kind of politics is judged by whether it provides true alternatives that are life-giving.

> Jesus embodies a kind of politics that is judged not by great ideas, party lines, or by meaning well.

The politics embodied by the Jesus movement cannot be confined to parties and certainly not to a two-party system that provides few real alternatives to the dominant state of affairs. The subject matter of politics is always bigger than party politics. Politics refers to the ordering of public life and of communities, which means that even political parties will have to be measured by what they contribute to public life and the communities they claim to serve. No politicians are ever home free based on party affiliations; rather they must be judged by a consistent track record of support for policies that are life-giving. As a result, any and all political projects remain subject to evaluation, not only from without but also from within its circle of supporters. Our politics do not need cheerleaders, religious or otherwise; we will "know them by their fruits" (Matt 7:16).

Religion and politics are always connected, whether we are aware of it or not, even though differences remain. The two are not two separate entities that run on parallel tracks. The strict separation of religion and politics is a modern Western idea that did not exist before modernity or outside of the Western world; neither Jesus nor Caesar would have been familiar with it. Some kind of relation of religion and politics is presupposed even by the principle of the separation of church and state that is anchored in the US Constitution. If there were no affinities between religion and politics it would make little sense to be concerned about transgressions between church and state, which today often find expression in corrupt alliances between church and party politics, particularly from the political Right.

The question is, therefore, not whether followers of Jesus should be engaged in politics in the broader sense of the word or not. Everything is political in the sense that it is linked to the ordering of public life—even the personal is political, as feminist thinkers have reminded us.[3] Withdrawal from politics altogether—a common effort in many faith communities—does not mean one is leaving politics behind; such a withdrawal usually amounts to endorsing dominant politics because it allows the respective state of affairs to prevail. So our question is not whether to engage in politics or not—"the church is not exempt from the difficult exercise of making political choices," as a South African theologian wrote during the days of Apartheid[4]—but what our politics will be. In what follows, the politics of race will serve as an example.

THE CONFLICT OF RELIGION AND POLITICS: NOT WHAT WE THOUGHT

What belongs to God? In a famous response to his opponents who questioned him about paying taxes to Caesar, Jesus's answer seems to affirm the modern assumption that religion and politics are separate matters. Jesus's solution to "give to the emperor the things that are the emperor's, and to God the things that are God's" (Mark 12:17) has often been understood in this way: "give to God the things that have to do with religion, give everything else to the emperor." In many churches, this is taken to mean "continue with the business of religion as usual and do not ever mention politics." In recent decades, this attitude has shifted from conservatives to liberals in the United States: while many conservatives from the 1950s to the 1970s would have stayed away from politics, today it is often liberal Christians who find fulfillment in personal spirituality and questions of the "meaning of life," while many conservative Christians are self-consciously engaged in faith-based politics.[5] Yet instead of shifting back and forth, we need to develop a more appropriate approach to both religion and politics.

The answers provided by modern Christianity (often shared by many modern scholars of religion) would not have made sense in the ancient world. First of all, religion and politics were inseparable, as were religion and economics. Second, for a Jewish person at the time of Jesus (and even today), the way Jesus frames things would have created a serious problem, because there is only one valid answer to the question of what belongs to God. Since God created heaven and earth, what belongs to God cannot be limited to religion, and neither can it be limited to religious communities or their property. What belongs to God, Jews and the early Christians would have agreed, is nothing less than everything.

So, if everything belongs to God, what belongs to Caesar? A deeper reading of the surprising conclusion of Jesus's response seems to be that nothing, really, belongs to Caesar.[6] What does that mean for paying taxes to Caesar? During his trial before Pilate, Jesus is accused of openly telling people not to pay taxes (Luke 23:2), yet the force of Jesus's response does not hinge on paying taxes per se. The force of the response lies in the reminder of the fundamental tension between God and Caesar and that the two are incompatible. This implies that resistance is an option, even though the form of resistance has to be spelled out and some ambiguity remains.

For people who live under the conditions of empire, paying taxes is not easily avoided, as it can amount to a matter of survival, of life and death. This is true for the Palestinian peasants and even their leaders, whom Jesus addresses, as well as for many people today. Miguel A. De La Torre, writing from a Latino immigrant perspective on the "politics of Jesús," sums it up this way: The question is "how to display compliance for survival's sake while disrupting the very social structures that create, force, and demand compliance."[7]

Those who asked the question about paying taxes would have been aware of the tension between God and Caesar, luring Jesus into a trap so that he would incriminate himself: openly rejecting the payment of taxes would have exposed him as a danger to Roman rule, affirming the payment of taxes would have exposed him as a traitor to the faith of Israel.[8] In framing the question this way, their own accommodation to the empire shines through. Most Romans, on the other hand, would not have noticed the tension between God and Caesar, because they would have assumed that God is on the side of Caesar, and that Caesar is on the side of God: paying taxes to one would, therefore, not be substantially different from tithing to the other. The same is true for Christians who switched to the side of the Roman Empire after Constantine and who saw God and the political and economic status quo on the same side.

The story in the Gospel of Mark hinges on the fact that Jesus's opponents understood the challenge he posed, even though he did not state it openly. To the Pharisees and the Herodians who asked the question about paying taxes it would not have occurred that religion and politics could be easily separated. Giving religion to God and everything else to Caesar—the way modern readers often resolve the tension—was not an option for them. Deep down, they also knew that the problem could not be solved by equating Caesar and God. More precisely, they knew that the people in the crowd would be aware of the difference between God and Caesar. In the older Jewish traditions, loyalty to God precluded loyalty to a king (see, for instance, 1 Sam 8:11-18). In the end, Jesus's response leaves them amazed, being confronted with a festering tension between Caesar and God that the dominant status quo would rather not address, but that could not be covered up forever. Jesus uncovers and highlights these tensions and takes the conversation to the next level.

This moment of surprise shows theology at its best. Unfortunately, throughout the centuries theology has often shaped up as the opposite of surprise, especially when it tried to ignore or reduce tensions and conflict, offering premature reconciliation. The politics of race illustrates what is at stake: open racism has been part of the history of both churches and nation, often supported by theological arguments. In the history of the United States, racism was not just a matter of prejudice but went hand-in-glove with the enslavement of millions of Africans, many of whom died in the so-called Middle Passage across the Atlantic Ocean, before even reaching their destination. There is now broad agreement that both racism that considers others less human and the enslavement of those others are wrong, and many churches have produced confessions of sin and apologies.[9]

With some exceptions, including prominent displays of prejudice in the era of Donald Trump's presidency, racism has often been pushed under the rug in the political and ecclesial realms in recent decades. This has sometimes made it appear as if the politics of God and the politics of Caesar have moved into alignment—as if all that had to be done was to give each its due. After the abolition of slavery in the nineteenth century, this meant to give to God whatever is God's and to Jim Crow what is Jim Crow's. After the civil rights movement this meant to give to God what is God's and to celebrate racial equality. However, if racism is defined not only as racial prejudice but more specifically as racial prejudice plus power, then it is necessary to deal with whatever power differentials between the races are still in place.

The ongoing conflict between Caesar and God will have to be addressed in all areas of life, including race relationships. Smoothing over this conflict produces not only distorted understandings of God and Caesar, it also perpetuates oppressive political relationships, even if they are merely at work under the surface.

> The ongoing conflict between Caesar and God will have to be addressed in all areas of life, including race relationships. Smoothing over this conflict produces not only distorted understandings of God and Caesar, it also perpetuates oppressive political relationships.

The discussion of the black Christ is a case in point. For centuries, Jesus was depicted in images taken from the dominant group that worshiped him. In Europe, images of Jesus presented a white Christ that bore the features of European Christians and their rulers. In this context, African American theologian James Cone presented his argument that Christ is black. His point was not, as is often mistakenly assumed, that all Christians should shape Christ in their own image. This is the approach of empire theology: just like the later Roman Empire envisioned Christ in terms of its emperors, with royal insignia, Christ has been envisioned in terms of dominant humanity ever since. Common European and US images depict Christ as light-haired and sometimes even blue-eyed. In this context, merely adding some images of Christ that resemble minorities does not present a challenge, especially if all of these images are considered equally valid. In this way, even pluralism and multiculturalism often help to shore up empires.

Talking about Christ as black, along the lines of Cone's argument, means that Jesus is found on the side of minorities, lives in solidarity with them and joins their struggles, and from there liberates everyone.[10] The black Christ challenges dominant images of Christ, just like Jesus challenged dominant images of the messiah and of God. White liberation theologian Frederick Herzog interprets Jesus's comment in the Gospel of John that we must be born again as "you must become black."[11]

This way of thinking about Christ brings us closer to the reality of Jesus as depicted in the Gospels, who was found on the side of people who experienced exploitation and oppression, who lived in solidarity with them and who joined their struggles. At stake, therefore, is not just a different kind of religion but also a different kind of politics: Caesar is to be resisted everywhere. The disciples apparently knew what was going on, as would all those who have experienced dominant power in their own bodies, including those who experience the presence of the resurrected Jesus in their lives today. Jesus emphasizes this knowledge in the following passage and offers an alternative: "You know that among the Gentiles those whom they recognize as their rulers lord it over them, and their great ones are tyrants over them. But it is not so among you; but whoever wishes to

39

become great among you must be your servant, and whoever wishes to be first among you must be slave of all. For the Son of Man came not to be served but to serve" (Mark 10:42-45a). Thus the tension between Jesus and Caesar continues.

WRONG GOD: WHAT DIFFERENCE DOES IT MAKE?

Perhaps the biggest problem with failing to distinguish between God and Caesar is that the work of God is envisioned in terms of existing relationships of power and the dominant status quo. In the previous chapter, we noted problems when God was thought of in the terms of classical theism as omnipotent and impassible. Now we can take a closer look at how this power manifests itself.

The conversation about paying taxes brings to light some of the political tensions. While many contemporaries in the United States resent paying taxes, a large part of our taxes goes toward improving the life of the community: infrastructure like roads and bridges are built with tax money; schools are provided as well as basic health care and benefits; cultural and community centers including parks, gardens, and swimming pools; environmental protection, foundational research, and so on.

In the ancient Roman Empire, while taxes likewise funded projects that benefited the community like roads and aqueducts, taxes were often used to shore up imperial structures that enabled the ruling class to further increase their already substantial wealth and power. One example would be building temples that promoted worship of the emperor and his accomplishments, which means that taxes also served a religious function, pulling together God and Caesar even more closely. Of course, substantial parts of tax revenues, then as now, are poured into the military, which has enjoyed the ongoing support of religion for two thousand years. In the year 150 CE, about 80 percent of the imperial budget went to the military; in 2015, the United States spent 54 percent of its discretionary budget on the military, which amounts to 37 percent of the total global spending on the military.[12]

In the Roman Empire, taxes were often burdensome, especially for its conquered subjects. In Galilee, taxes affected especially the peasant population, which was taxed several times by representatives of the empire.[13] In this case, it makes little difference that Galileans (unlike Judeans) paid taxes to the warlords of the Roman Empire rather than to the empire itself.[14] Due to heavy tax burdens, many peasants were driven off their lands because they had to go into debt to pay their taxes and at some point were no longer able to service their debts. The politics of taxation was, therefore, not just a nuisance but a matter of life and death for entire peasant communities whose way of life was disrupted and ultimately destroyed.

At stake, therefore, is not just the politics of taxation but what paying taxes to Caesar amounted to in the lives of Jesus's contemporaries. While we will look at the economic implications of the tax system in a later chapter, here we are interested in the political implications. As Richard Horsley has observed, the Roman authorities and their affiliates, both warlords like Herod and religious representatives like elite priests, were not interfering directly in the village communities as long as they paid taxes and tributes.[15] Heavy taxes and tributes were, therefore, a primary means of political control that assured that village communities would not become too powerful and gain the ability to determine their own lives.

The politics of taxation was, therefore, not merely another institution of the Roman Empire; taxation was the primary way in which the heavy burdens of the empire were placed on the least of these in order to control them. Here, the politics of Jesus provides an alternative. Refusing to sanction the use of the subjugated population's resources for the purpose of servicing the empire, Jesus opens the way for a different kind of relationship. Today, African American communities continue in the tradition of Jesus when they draw attention to how tax dollars are used for policing minorities, for instance through racial profiling and mass incarceration, rather than for the welfare of the community. Following the god of Caesar is not merely a matter of bad theology!

Of course, there are differences between then and now. For the most part, taxes today do not get people into irreconcilable debt, as they did in the times of Jesus; taxes are rarely sanctioned by divine fiat, and taxes are not used for religious purposes (although we should not forget about tax breaks for religious organizations). What is more likely to get people into debt today are low wages and, related to the inability to make ends meet, predatory lending services.[16]

Nevertheless, some of the more recent tax laws in the United States mirror the principles of the Roman Empire—supporting the interests of wealth and power by constantly lowering taxes at the top, making the broader population shoulder much of the cost of businesses, and even funneling a significant portion of the tax revenue to the top through what has become known as "corporate welfare."[17] As of January 1, 2018, the official tax rate for corporations has been lowered from 35 percent to 21 percent, the lowest rate since the Great Depression.[18] Some of the justification appears to be similar as well, based on the belief that if the ruling classes are doing better everyone will be doing better.

At the heart of all of these policies is not money but power. Several assumptions appear to be at work that are modeled on images of a god who resembles Caesar more than Jesus: First, there is the assumption that those who exercise top-down power provide the best hope for people and the world, an assumption that is widely shared not only in the ancient world but also today, across the political spectrum. Party politics seems to agree on this point, as Republicans, Democrats, and even Ralph Nader (for a brief moment) have gone to bat for this assumption.[19] Second, there is an assumption that those who exercise top-down power backed by wealth are doing so in ways that are mostly benevolent. A few bad apples, like Kenneth Lay, the CEO who brought down Enron, are usually seen as the exception, not the rule. Supporting this sort of logic is one sense of what many people think "giving to Caesar what is Caesar's" really means. How could "giving to God what is God's" model a different way?

WRONG GOD, RIGHT GOD: THE STRUGGLE CONTINUES

Jesus, as we have seen, seems to imply that everything belongs to God. This means that no political status quo can ever have the final word and that any political approach must remain subject to questioning—the same is true for religion. As a result, Caesar is not in charge, God is. But what might it mean to consider God to be "in charge"?

The thrust of this theological insight led to another conflict as history went on. In the Middle Ages, popes and emperors challenged each other as to who was in charge. The popes, seeing themselves as representatives of Jesus while aspiring to imperial power, assumed that they were in charge. Emperors like Charlemagne and later emperors who fashioned themselves in his image, on the other hand, assumed that the Holy Roman Empire had been put in their trust. Whichever way the pendulum swung, the outcome was not subsantially different: highly powerful rulers from the realms of politics and religion claimed to be the representatives of God, often resulting in theocratic nightmares.

One such nightmare played itself out in the Conquest of the Americas, when Spain and Portugal took possession of another continent, endorsed by the close cooperation of church and crown. This put both of them squarely on the side of Caesar. In 1493, one year after Columbus landed in the Americas, Pope Alexander VI issued a bull that granted Spain the exclusive rights to the lands discovered by Columbus and all others yet to be discovered in this part of the world. The occupation of the land, and the enslavement and subsequent genocide of tens of millions of indigenous peoples was the catastrophic result.[20] Even the milder colonialism suggested by the Spanish Dominican friar Bartolomé de Las Casas in opposition to the Spanish Conquest (practiced to some degree by later Northern European colonizers) did not change the dominant flow of power.[21]

Racism was a fundamental part of the problem, as those who were not of European descent were generally seen as less than fully human. Las Casas's efforts to lift up the indigenous population, comparing them favorably to the ancient Romans and Greeks, still preserved a racial hierarchy because the Spanish were considered even more advanced. This racial taxonomy persisted, even as Las Casas later repented of his efforts to replace Amerindian slaves with African slaves, whom he considered even more inferior.[22]

The heart of the problem was the assumption that there was no real difference between the rule of the emperors, the rule of the popes, and the rule of God. Ruling—"being in charge"—meant that power was exercised from the top down, from places of privilege and prestige, wielded over the masses in ways that were sometimes more—and sometimes less—benevolent. Political and religious power, while distinct to some degree in terms of its function (the pope authorized the emperors in Latin America), shared the imperial ethos of operating from above, just as God was seen as operating from above. According to a common and tragic misunderstanding, this is shored up by what theologians have often called a "Christology from above." Yet if God is not envisioned as "above" but as at work among the people, following the life and ministry of Christ, even a Christology that proceeds from Christ's divinity can no longer be called a "Christology from above."

Moreover, even benevolent forms of top-down power, claimed by many of the later European empires and the United States in contradistinction to the Spanish Conquest, are deeply problematic. To be sure, some options were better than others. There is a nominal difference between enslaving people and working them to death, as the Spaniards did with the indigenous populations, and enslaving people and taking care of them to some degree (like livestock), as the plantation owners in the United States did with the African slaves. Yet these forms of slavery were closely related and based on distorted theological ideas of how God is "in charge" of creation, the God-given superiority of Europeans and Americans, and what was considered natural law.

Las Casas, opposing enslavement and the harsh subordination of the indigenous population, promoted what he considered the way of Jesus Christ as the "only way." Instead of the coercive forms of evangelization practiced by the Roman Catholic missionaries, he advocated a "gentle, coaxing, gracious way" and the "gentle persuasion" of the "culture of

44

Christ."[23] Yet the assumption of the superiority of the Spanish Empire and of the Roman Catholic Church secured the continued domination of Spain in the New World, however benign and nonviolent Las Casas might have envisioned it.

All these approaches are in tension with the politics of Jesus, which rejected any form of top-down power and endorsed the power of service, as we have already seen (Mark 10:42-44). And more than one scholar notes that the alternative to top-down power is not detached spirituality but servanthood. Yet servanthood itself can be a problematic term, especially if it somehow endorses submissive relationships elsewhere.[24] Jesus's challenge to the rulers who "show off their authority over them" rejects top-down power once and for all, opening up new relationships of mutuality that do not allow for the reproduction of dominant power. In other words, the perversions of the relationship of master and slave are not merely relieved but relinquished.

The politics of Jesus, in tension with the politics of Caesar, is not a way of making masters more kind and slaves less rebellious; the politics of Jesus puts an end to slavery and completely reshapes the relationships of top and bottom, up and down, master and slave, deconstructing the relations of ruling and subaltern classes throughout history. In the Gospel of Matthew, Jesus reminds his followers that they have only one teacher, therefore all are brothers and sisters (Matt 23:8).[25]

> The politics of Jesus, in tension with the politics of Caesar, is not a way of making masters more kind and slaves less rebellious; the politics of Jesus puts an end to slavery and completely reshapes the relationships of top and bottom, up and down, master and slave, deconstructing the relations of ruling and subaltern classes throughout history.

This brings us back to the earlier observation that loyalty to God precluded loyalty to kings in the past. Richard Horsley, in a tongue-in-cheek manner, puts it this way: "Israel was, with regard to YHWH, a theocracy, but with regard to concrete social practice, it was what might be called a cooperative anarchy."[26] Human relationships, in other words, are not determined by top-down power: the model is cooperation rather than subordination. However, what might be meant by the word *theocracy*, the rule of God, in this context? This word tends to arouse strong emotions and a good deal of confusion, scaring many contemporaries to death and awakening sentiments of triumphalism in others.

When God in 1 Samuel 8:11-17 opposes the rule of kings, the king is portrayed as the one who enslaves people:

> He will take your sons and appoint them to his chariots and to be his horsemen, and to run before his chariots; and he will appoint for himself commanders of thousands and commanders of fifties, and some to plow his ground and to reap his harvest, and to make his implements of war and the equipment of his chariots. He will take your daughters to be perfumers and cooks and bakers. He will take the best of your fields and vineyards and olive orchards and give them to his courtiers. He will take one-tenth of your grain and of your vineyards and give it to his officers and his courtiers. He will take your male and female slaves, and the best of your cattle and donkeys, and put them to his work. He will take one-tenth of your flocks, and you shall be his slaves.

Whatever the word *theocracy* might mean, this cannot be it, God does not function like a king or a traditional ruler who is "in charge." Theocracy here amounts to the refusal of subordination!

In order to determine the power and rule of God, we will have to take another look at how Jesus embodies power in the world. What is clear is that Jesus did not seek to imitate the power of Caesar and his representatives; but neither did Jesus call for forms of resistance against empire that would mimic top-down power. There is broad agreement that Jesus was not a Zealot or a member of the Sicarii, elite groups that organized armed and violent resistance struggles against the Romans. This observation is often misused, however, as if the fact that Jesus was not a Zealot meant that he had no interest in embracing power and resisting empire.

Recent research has reminded us what Americans who remember the civil rights movement should know, namely that there are alternative forms of resistance that do not have to employ the top-down methods of the status quo, like terror and armed violence.[27] In fact, then and now nonviolent popular protests have often proven to be more powerful and more challenging to the power of Caesar than violent attacks. In the case of the civil rights movement, racial supremacy and the economic exploitation of African Americans were successfully challenged by nonviolent methods of resistance that proved more powerful than the violence that was encountered by the movement.[28]

One thing we know is that the Jesus movement, however limited it might have been in its own time, was successful enough to pose a challenge to the dominant powers. Jesus must have presented a real threat to Caesar, which is the reason why he had to be contained and eliminated. Many others at the time who were simply radical preachers, like a certain Jesus son of Hananiah, were beaten and reprimanded but not crucified.[29]

RIGHT GOD: "YOUR KINGDOM COME"

The first petition of the Lord's Prayer (Matt 6:10) reads: "Your kingdom come. Your will be done, on earth as it is in heaven." Jesus's politics are as comprehensive as can be: God's will is for heaven—of course—but it is also for the earth. God's kingdom, thus, applies to heaven and earth in the same way.

But why use political terms like *kingdom* when such terms could get people in trouble with existing kingdoms, and when other terms would have been readily available?[30] It stands to reason that Jesus does not use this term naively, without consideration, but in order to present a clear contrast to the dominant kingdom and its representatives in his time. This is a dangerous move, as even the mere act of praying for God's kingdom amounts to a challenge of any and all existing political systems.[31]

47

Unfortunately, churches have often compromised this challenge of God's kingdom by reducing it to what has been understood as religion in modernity: the realms of the private, the family, particular communities of interest—in short, to anything that is not part of the broader political scene. French theologian Alfred Loisy noted the irony in his famous remark that while Jesus proclaimed God's kingdom, what came was the church.[32] Reclaiming Jesus's political challenge to Caesar, what do we do about God's kingdom, and what is its promise and potential? And what is the role of the church?

Before taking a closer look at the positive meaning of the term *God's kingdom*, we must note two problems. As Crossan has pointed out, translating the Greek term *basileia* as *kingdom* often produces false ideas of kings and static locations.[33] In Jesus's use of the term, dominant notions of kings and fixed, unchanging locations are deconstructed. In addition, talking about God's kingdom tends to invoke certain ideas of theocracy according to which God rules like a king, from the top down. These ideas look surprisingly similar to the role of Caesar in the Roman Empire. Once again, we need to remind ourselves of the contrast between Jesus and Caesar.

Two examples provide images of God's kingdom that are diametrically opposed to the kingdom of Caesar. Here, dominant notions of kings and of theocracy are thoroughly deconstructed and reconstructed. In the temptation stories at the beginning of the Gospels of Luke and Matthew (Matt 4:8-10; Luke 4:5-8), Jesus categorically rejects the kind of top-down power that was characteristic of the Roman Empire and of virtually all other empires since. Here is the version from Matthew:

> Again, the devil took him to a very high mountain and showed him all the kingdoms of the world and their splendor; and he said to him, "All these I will give you, if you will fall down and worship me." Jesus said to him, "Away with you, Satan! for it is written,
>
> *"Worship the Lord your God, and serve only him."*

What is it that Jesus declines? At first sight, it is worship of Satan, rather than power over all the kingdoms of the earth. But why would this be a temptation if Jesus were to expect God to give him this power only a short time later? Being king over all empires by the grace of God would have been preferable anyway. It seems that what Jesus rejected, therefore, was not just worship of the devil in exchange for top-down power, but top-down power altogether. In other words, Jesus refuses to be a king like Caesar. However, if God's kingdom proclaimed by Jesus is not characterized by top-down power, we have to rethink what politics looks like. Jesus's politics leaves no room for triumphalistic ideas of theocracy.

> What Jesus rejected, therefore, was not just worship of the devil in exchange for top-down power, but top-down power altogether. In other words, Jesus refuses to be a king like Caesar.

Another interpretation of God's kingdom comes from the theologies of the African American slaves. When the term *kingdom* or *God's kingdom* is used in the spirituals, it is unlikely that the slaves were envisioning a kingdom like that of their masters, where power flows once again unilaterally from the top down, accompanied by the crack of a whip.

Here is the first stanza of "Ain't that Good News":

I got a crown up in-a that kingdom,
Ain't-a that good news!
I got a crown up in-a that kingdom,
Ain't-a that good news!
I'm-a gonna lay down this world,
gonna to shoulder up-a my cross,
Gonna to take it home-a to my Jesus,
Ain't-a that good news![34]

Here is a vision of a new world where all people are valued. Instead of the top-down rule of one king, the slaves are now kings wearing crowns and all have power. And what might look like hope for another world really is hope for this world here and now, as talking about heaven was a common way for the spirituals to throw off their masters who would never have tolerated the political implications of what was said. Once again, God's kingdom is reenvisioned here in powerful ways that are at once religious and political. Even though the slaves believed that God was in charge, the theocracy of Caesar or of the slave-masters has no room here; God rules in a different way that allows them to "lay down this world," that is, to bring an end to this world and its oppressive politics and to bring in a new world of freedom.

Keep in mind that neither the African American slaves nor the early Christians had any direct access to political power. In a world where holding public political office or participating in politics at the official level was not an option for most people, politics had to do with embodying alternative ways of life and forming alternative relationships and communities. Early Christianity's challenges to the kingdom of Caesar manifested themselves not only in ideas and thought but in alternative ways of life that were public and for all to see. This was their contribution to politics. Following Jesus, therefore, was always a political statement and never merely a religious one.

For contemporary Christians this means that voting Republican or Democrat is not the only way of participating in politics, which comes as a relief given the current state of affairs and the fact that the vote can always be manipulated. Embracing alternative ways of life, like the early Christians and the African American slaves, may indeed be a much more significant contribution to politics than most people realize. This would not only be a powerful witness to the politics of Jesus and God's kingdom, but it would also enable followers of Jesus to hold the feet of any political party to the fire, especially the one for which they voted.

This brings us back to Jesus and helps us understand his ministry in a broader sense. As we noted, what made Jesus so dangerous to the Roman Empire and its powerbrokers that they finally had to execute him was that he was not merely a radical preacher but rather someone who embodied the power of God in alternative ways.[35] As recent research has made clear, Jesus was an organizer who was able to inspire people to become part of social movements and to build power by strengthening their relationships and

50

their networks.[36] This would become even clearer if we translated traditional terms like *making disciples* into *organizing* or *building community power*. With Jesus, ministry itself turns into a form of organizing the community.

Keep in mind, however, that the politics of Jesus, proclaiming God's kingdom and organizing for it, does not singlehandedly create a movement *ex nihilo*, from nothing, as the theologians say. Jesus was deeply rooted in the traditions and communities of his time. His context was the village communities of his time, which were in danger of falling apart due to the burdens placed on them by the Roman Empire and its vassals. These communities were tied together by communal interest projects as well as by communal prayers, both rooted in popular Israelite traditions.[37]

Just as Jesus built on and developed these traditions and relationships, in order to pursue the politics of Jesus we need to ask where we might find communities and movements that are already in place or emerging. Rather than trying to reinvent the wheel, we need to take a closer look at the potential of our faith communities and other existing community organizations. These organizations are not limited to what is narrowly considered to be "religious" but include all those who have a track record of engaging in life-giving politics, like black churches and some of the holiness traditions, including movements like Black Lives Matter and Occupy Wall Street (morphed into Occupy Sandy and Occupy Homes), civil rights and immigrant rights organizations such as the Dreamers, and—dare I say it—labor unions.[38]

CONCLUSION: RECLAIMING THE POLITICS OF JESUS

The way we envision the politics of Jesus—*God's kingdom* and even related concepts of *theocracy*—looks radically different from the politics of Caesar at every turn. The result is what has been called a "contrast society"[39] in which the God of Jesus does not rule from the top down—conveniently located in heaven or other high places—but is at work on the ground, in the formation of alternative communities whose way of life does not aim at overpowering others but at inviting them into shared relations of power. The politics of Jesus functions, thus, not via coercion but attraction. The attraction at work here is not the one that is at work in hierarchical relationships where those at the top capture the desire of the multitude—something both conservatives and liberals dream of—the attraction at work here is based on the formation of real alternatives to the dominant way of life.[40] Instead of being manipulated by the desire of the dominant, the people themselves become agents.[41]

Just like faith in the wrong god went hand in hand with the powers of empire, which often turned deadly for those on its margins (whether they were subject to military or cultural pressures, or tax burdens that would push them off their family lands and into poverty), faith in the God of Jesus Christ went hand in hand with another way of life and another politcs.[42] This way of life was focused on the well-being of all members of the community, rather than merely individual families and their members ("Who are my mother and my brothers?" Mark 3:33). It also included the least of these, not primarily as objects of welfare but in places of honor ("the last will be first," Matt 20:16), and it sought to bring about the kingdom (or *kindom*, to use a less empire-determined phrase[43]) of God rather than the kingdom of Caesar. History never repeats itself in exactly the same way, of course, but today this faith and way of life again calls North American Christians to choose the God of Jesus over the forces of empire.

QUESTIONS FOR REFLECTION AND DISCUSSION

1. Should followers of Jesus be concerned about politics? Why or why not?

2. How does the dominant politics of empire manifest itself today, and how are the churches part of what is going on, consciously and unconsciously?

3. What difference might communities of faith make in the world of politics broadly conceived? Can you think of some positive historical examples?

Chapter 3
THE MATERIALISM OF RELIGION

On Religion and Things That Matter

Failure to understand the tension between life-giving and malignant religion has caused many to exchange their connectedness to the earth and its inhabitants for the proverbial pie in the sky. While this has gone on for centuries, the challenges to global survival are becoming more urgent every moment. The seriousness of our situation goes beyond anything seen in the past, as millions of human lives could be wiped out, either by the tools of modern warfare or by the consequences of climate change. Cautious estimates by the World Health Organization expect two hundred fifty thousand additional deaths per year between 2030 and 2050 due to climate change.[1] These estimates do not take into account the snowball effect, which means that the climate is likely to spin out of control faster and faster as time goes by.

How are followers of Jesus to respond? What is the role of religion and spirituality in the material world, where the survival of millions of people and the planet must be worked out? Simply denying climate change or other challenges to humanity, based on the fact that there is not 100 percent agreement, is hardly an option. If an individual were diagnosed with a medical condition and then got second and third opinions to the point

53

that 97 percent of experts agreed (as is the case with climate change)[2], would that person not be compelled to take action?

Since the religion of Caesar has always had a firm foot in the material world, it is not threatened by religions limiting themselves to non-material and spiritual other worlds. In the Roman Empire, the so-called mystery religions and gnostic groups promoted the focus on other worlds. In gnostic theologies the material world was considered evil or of secondary importance, and the goal of religion was to leave the material world behind and to swing up to higher spheres. In these otherworldly theologies, Jesus and Caesar never really meet because they are found in different worlds. Mystery religions usually allowed for membership in various different groups as well as adherence to the imperial religion at the same time.[3] This leaves Caesar in control of the material world.

Today, there are many efforts to direct Christian attention away from this world. Best-selling interpretations of the idea of a "rapture" (an interpretation of a single biblical verse in Thessalonians 4:17) assume that Christians will be lifted out of the world at a specific time to come.[4] Predictions for the end of the world are a dime a dozen, constantly revised and updated because none of them ever get the date right. Yet this is only the tip of the iceberg. Plenty of other theologies promise a pie in the sky, and not all of them are found in conservative theological camps.

New age ideas and some liberal spiritual developments have also contributed to directing people of faith away from this world. Even well-meaning moral critiques of "materialism" and "consumerism" are misleading people if they forget that the solution is not to give up the material world for the spiritual but to change it.[5] These are not inconsequential interpretations of Christianity, as the collective lack of attention to the world by people who claim Jesus has done tremendous damage to the earth and its people.

Jesus's life and ministry stand in stark contrast to world-denying and anti-material theologies. Even the Gospel of John, often considered less interested in material things than the other Gospels, clashes with world-denying theologies. Even though John can sound like the anti-material theologies of gnosticism, the very beginning of the Gospel affirms material reality. After introducing the idea of *the word* (Greek: *logos*), which gnostics assumed was about spiritual things rather than material ones, John states: "The Word became flesh and lived among us" (John 1:14). Here gnostic terms like *the word* are turned around and grounded in material reality. The word, according to John, is not about a spiritual over against a material reality. In Jesus, the word materializes in the life of a person who is standing with both feet on the ground.

> The difference between Jesus and Caesar is that we are dealing with two very different material realities and two very different spiritualities.

The difference between Jesus and Caesar is, therefore, not that one would be interested in material reality and the other in spiritual things. The difference is that we are dealing with two very different material realities and two very different spiritualities. The Gospels portray a very material Jesus, written at a time in the history of early Christianity when faith was in danger of withdrawing from the world. In the Synoptic Gospels of Matthew, Mark, and Luke, Jesus is closely related not only to the world but to the particular struggles of everyday life. In the Gospel of John, too, Jesus is found in the struggles of life. In contrast to other prophetic movements of his time, including the Qumran communities, Jesus does not lead people into the wilderness; instead, he sends his disciples into the villages, where his ministry is rooted.[6]

THE CONFLICT OF THE MATERIAL AND THE SPIRITUAL: NOT WHAT WE THOUGHT

That we have become "too materialistic" is a complaint often heard today. This means, supposedly, that people care too much about material things and about getting more stuff. Similar critiques have also been leveled against the so-called Prosperity Gospel, which promises its adherents fabulous material abundance in this life. But what is the alternative? Would the remedy be to become more spiritual, and what might this even mean?

Jesus, taking a leaf from the Hebrew prophets, has a different suggestion. When John the Baptist asks the famous question whether Jesus is the one who is to come or whether they should wait for another, Jesus responds by pointing to the transformation of material reality. Rather than talking about otherworldly realities or about the future, Jesus notes what is already happening, namely that people are being healed, the dead raised, and "and the poor have good news brought to them" (Matt 11:3-5). Why go through all this trouble of listing examples of material transformation? Would it not have been easier for Jesus to promise otherworldly fulfillment, like that the sick will be going to heaven and that the dead are already there? And why bring up good news to the poor? Is that not the most material claim of all, as promising the poor that they will go to heaven after they die would not really be good news to them here and how? Does not good news to the poor mean something like "you will no longer be poor"?

From this passage, which is nothing less than a manifesto of the work of Jesus, it is clear that Jesus's ministry is squarely rooted in that material world; rather than leaving the world to the powers of the Roman Empire, Jesus values it, deals with it, and transforms it. The same is true for what we might call spiritual reality or spirituality. Jesus does not leave spirituality to the high priests of the Roman Empire or to the Judaism of the powerful that had made their own arrangement with the empire. Rather, Jesus's spirituality transforms the world, as we see in the Lord's Prayer: hallowing God's name is linked with eating bread and forgiving debt (see below). With Jesus, both the material and the spiritual work together for the good, contributing to the flourishing of all life.

> It is clear that Jesus's ministry is squarely rooted in that material world; rather than leaving the world to the powers of the Roman Empire, Jesus values it, deals with it, and transforms it.

How is any of this different from the Gospel of Prosperity? The wealth produced via the Prosperity Gospel follows the principles of capitalism, where winner takes all and some get fabulously wealthy—often on the backs of others. Even when the Gospel of Prosperity encourages the development of small businesses, these businesses are based on the logic of capitalism rather than the logic of Jesus, as the primary focus tends to be on the accomplishments of the entrepreneurs rather than on the community. As with neoliberal capitalism, the Gospel of Prosperity assumes that if the wealthy are doing better, all are doing better.

The problem here is not with a focus on material reality, wealth, and business; the problem is with who ultimately benefits. Although the Gospel of Prosperity preaches its message to all, in the end only a few are benefiting from it. The preachers, of course, are prospering and so are a few church members, but it is hard to see how growing wealth at the top is able to raise whole communities out of poverty. Worse yet, the logic of the Gospel of Prosperity puts the blame on those who are not able to make it: their faith is not deep enough and their commitment is not strong enough.

The logic of Jesus functions differently. Instead of trying to build wealth and power at the top, Jesus supports wealth and power in the community. Jesus proclaims God's kingdom to the multitude, many of them peasants, who are indebted and hungry, and for whom the petitions of the Lord's Prayer for bread and debt relief have a deeply material meaning.[7] Rather than playing spiritual and material things off against each other, the spiritual gains new depth here, as it contributes to the transformation of the world.

Compare this relation of spiritual and material to what is commonly criticized with the term *materialism*. Material things are closely linked to non-material ones. The new cell phone, for instance, promises relationships and access to others who might hear us and follow us; more than the mere desire to own more stuff, what sells cell phones is hope for happiness and love. The same is true also for the new car: the material reality of an automobile is deeply tied up with promises of safety, functionality, comfort, status, and mobility.

The tension is, therefore, not between material and spiritual but between what kind of material realities and what kind of spiritual realities we value, and how the material and the spiritual are related in each case. The material realities that Jesus values are linked to people's needs, which extend from food to freedom from debt and from temptation, according to the Lord's Prayer. The material realities for which Caesar stands, on the other hand, are linked to inordinate desires for fabulous wealth and power over others, also reflected in the proclamation of the Gospel of Prosperity. When Jesus challenges fabulous wealth and the related power over others—recall the playful image of the impossibility of a camel going through the eye of a needle (Mark 11:23-27)—he does not reject material reality as such but particular embodiments of it.

Similar things can be said about the spirituality that Jesus values as it, too, is linked to people's needs rather than to the inordinate desires of the rulers. Jesus models an economy of prayer that does not consist in publicly heaping up "empty phrases" and making "many words" (Matt 6:5-8) but in praying for the things that really matter in life, spelled out in the Lord's Prayer (Matt 6:9-13). In this way, the spirituality of Jesus differs fundamentally from the spirituality of Caesar and the powerful.

While the Synoptic Gospels combine the material and spiritual, the Gospel of John sometimes appears to be playing them off against each other. In the conversation between Jesus and Nicodemus, for instance, there are stark contrasts between flesh and spirit (John 3:6), heaven and earth (John 3:12), and salvation and condemnation (John 3:17). Another look at these passages, however, shows a surprising commitment to life in this world: God "loves the world" and gives "eternal life" (John 3:16), an expression that refers to not perishing and to not being condemned. All this is happening in the present world, according to the Johannine Jesus, rather than merely in the future or after death. Likewise, the judgment is taking place in the present world as well, as those who do not follow Jesus "are condemned already," love "darkness rather than light," and do evil deeds (John 3:18-19). The stark contrasts in the Gospel of John are, therefore, not drawn between material and spiritual reality or between heaven and earth; the lines are drawn between good and evil deeds (John

3:20-21). What is important about eternal life in the Gospel of John is that it starts here and now—that it continues after death is taken for granted.

> What is important about eternal life in the Gospel of John is that it starts here and now—that it continues after death is taken for granted.

According to an often-quoted statement attributed to the French theologian Pierre Teilhard de Chardin, "We are not human beings having a spiritual experience; we are spiritual beings having a human experience."[8] Jesus does not split up reality like this. The Lord's Prayer brings together heaven and earth, and people are not divided into spiritual first and human second.

WRONG GOD: WHAT DIFFERENCE DOES IT MAKE?

Neglect of the material concerns of Jesus comes in many shapes and forms. Many theologians still follow the conclusions of Albert Schweitzer in 1906 that material reality and the present were only of limited interest to Jesus because he assumed that the world would end soon.[9] This often amounts to a particular form of "giving to Caesar what is Caesar's": Caesar gets the world, and God gets whatever remains after the end of the world.

Even those who see Jesus mainly as a wisdom teacher are not always claiming the full material impact of Jesus's ministry, as they sometimes limit the reality of God that Jesus represents to intellectual or moral frameworks. Jesus's pacifism, for instance, is presented as a good idea that is then pitted against the idea of war; what is missing is a consideration of the material embodiment of this pacifism in the messiness of everyday life. The trouble with these kinds of approaches is that they still give too much credit to Caesar, who runs the world while Jesus produces great ideas that await embodiment, rather than alternative ways of life.

These problems are compounded by otherworldly interpretations of the work of Jesus that have captured large parts of the popular imagination. The question "Are you saved?" that is commonly asked in Christian circles in the South of the United States usually refers to whether people think they will go to heaven after they die. In this case, salvation is a matter of life after death rather than life before death. Jesus has to do with the former; the latter is left to the status quo, which is determined by Caesar. John Wesley encountered these interpretations already in eighteenth-century England and commented that what happens after death was not the most important question: a better question regarding salvation, according to Wesley, was how salvation was expressed in people's lives here and now.[10]

The related question about whether someone has accepted Jesus as their "personal lord and savior" betrays similar attitudes. When religion is considered mostly an otherworldly affair, terms like *lord* and *savior* lose the political undertones that early Christians heard, as religion and politics were not separate entities for them. And even when religion is not pushed off into another world altogether, it often is still limited to private affairs, emphasizing the personal realm. Thus, people might consider Jesus as a personal hero, a moral example, and perhaps even a great congregational leader. But all these approaches still leave running the world to Caesar. Such understandings are widespread and are common in both conservative and liberal theological camps.[11]

Popular takes on the rapture (then and now) demonstrate some of the problems with otherworldly understandings of religion. The contemporary Left Behind book series by authors Tim LaHaye and Jerry B. Jenkins has sold millions and millions of copies and depicts the rapture as a moment in time when individuals are taken up into heaven. This leads to chaos, as airplanes are left without pilots, cars without drivers, trains without conductors, and families and communities without some of their members. The whole idea is based on an obscure reference in 1 Thessalonians 4:17 about the faithful who will "meet with the Lord in the air," together with those who have died.[12]

60

This interpretation of the rapture implies a divine disconnect with the things of this world, and it has consequences. When interpreted by those who experience life as a struggle, like for the African American slaves, the message might perhaps be that "trouble don't last always," as one of the Spirituals puts it. When interpreted by people who enjoy some privilege and power, on the other hand, the message often tends to be one of securing their status and disregarding the world and other people. Of course, when Christians neglect the material world and its people, others will take care of it for them, as a vacuum never lasts long. Thus, those in power—whether a Caesar or a US president—will have free rein in matters material.

Talking about God only in terms of things spiritual and otherworldly creates other theological problems. When sin is understood as pride, for instance, it makes a difference if persons actually embody pride in their lives or not. For Caesar, for instance, pride is not only an occasional spiritual attitude but an entire way of life. By the same token, a person who is forced to work hard to make ends meet and to fight for survival is less likely to be driven by the sin of pride. When an awareness of this difference is lacking, it is not uncommon that the sin of pride and the virtue of humility are proclaimed to those who are experiencing humiliation every day, while those who are the epitome of pride will never hear a sermon on the topic.[13]

Similar problems occur with affirmations of a divine covenant. When this biblical theme, rooted both in the Old and New Testaments, is proclaimed in otherworldly terms, the result is often an elitist attitude of those who feel they alone have been chosen by God for better things. As the concern for the real world disappears, the communities of the faithful become self-centered—who would not know of a few narcissistic churches? Yet the covenants between God and Israel, which Jesus picks up and broadens, have everything to do with life in this world and with the many rather than the few. God's covenants with Abraham, with Noah, and with Moses, for instance, are about the flourishing of life on this earth. The thought of going to heaven after death is not even mentioned—the idea itself occurs very late in the writings of the Hebrew Bible and when Jesus picks it up, it is tied to the transformation of the world.

At the center of Jesus's teaching, as recent research has pointed out, is the renewal of the covenant between God and Israel at Mount Sinai.[14] This particular concern for the covenant was set in the context of peasant villages whose common bonds were challenged by outside pressures, in particular taxes and tributes. In this context, reinforcing the solidarity of the villagers against those who exploited them—not only from the outside but also from the inside by charging interest and trying to gain control of others' possessions—became a matter of survival.[15] In this situation, covenant theology—often seen as a matter of otherworldly interests—makes a real difference in the lives of people, reaffirming the difference between Jesus and Caesar.

Otherworldly theology tends to overlook key themes in the Jewish and Christian traditions, like for instance an emphasis on the land that is central in the traditions of Israel on which Jesus draws. Yet when things are overlooked they often return through the back door. This is particularly true for the land. According to a famous observation by Kenyan Prime Minister and President Jomo Kenyatta, "When the missionaries came to Africa they had the Bible and we had the land. They said 'Let us pray.' We closed our eyes. When we opened them, we had the Bible and they had the land."[16] Otherwordly theology tends to have serious and often detrimental material consequences.

Other accounts of how land changed hands in the context of missions tell a more nuanced story but the outcome is the same. In the missions to the Native Americans in the United States, for instance, the missionaries often did not gain personally from the exploitation of the people and their land. This means that it is very likely that their concern for otherworldly matters was sincere. Yet, tragically, this concern for otherworldly matters was part of the problem, as their missionary work enabled others to exploit Native Americans and to take their land.[17] One way this could have been prevented would have been to learn from Jesus's emphasis on material reality, everyday life, and a comprehensive covenant with God that includes the material world.

WRONG GOD, RIGHT GOD:
THE STRUGGLE CONTINUES

When the Spirituals of the African American slaves are used in the worship of white mainline churches, they sometimes sound like they would proclaim an otherworldly reality, favoring heaven over the earth. This picks up on a long history. When the slaves sang "Swing low, sweet chariot, coming for to carry me home," for instance, the masters heard a yearning for heaven as a place far removed from the earth. The slaves, on the other hand, heard the good news of the Underground Railroad that would take them to freedom.

The so-called "Spirituals" thus promote a spirituality that is grounded in real life, subverting the false spirituality of the masters who were happy for the slaves to engage religion as an otherworldly matter and to go to heaven after death. At stake here are not just two different theologies and two different spiritualities—at stake are also two very different Gods.

> At stake here are not just two different theologies and two different spiritualities— at stake are also two very different Gods.

The holiness traditions that took off in the eighteenth and nineteenth centuries share a similar emphasis on religion as relevant for life in this world. The concern for sanctification, typical for holiness traditions, was linked to a spirituality that found expression on the ground. And even when the focus was mostly on the personal sanctification of the individual, individual concerns were always embedded in the community to some degree. The prohibition against drinking hard liquor, characteristic of many holiness movements, for instance, was not just a matter of personal abstinence but also a matter of strengthening families and—in the case of John Wesley—a matter of preserving the limited resources of grain for food rather than for the distilling of alcohol.[18] In the United States, moreover, the early holiness traditions were often racially inclusive, bringing together both European Americans and African Americans.

The down-to-earth spirituality of holiness can be seen, for instance, in Wesley's pragmatic interpretation of Jesus's admonition not to store treasures on earth but in heaven because "where your treasure is, there your heart will be also" (Matt 6:19-21). For Wesley, storing treasures in heaven simply means giving to the poor.[19] This is in stark contrast to otherworldly religion, where storing treasures in heaven usually means giving money to the church or—in the cases of the Gospel of Prosperity—giving large amounts of money to the pastors who frequently travel in private jets and inhabit expansive mansions. To be sure, when churches are the recipients of the treasures of the faithful, they often spend part of their funds on the community, but the priorities are reversed.

In the famous story of the "Widow's Mite" according to the Gospel of Luke (21:1-4) the tension between the true God and the false god shines through. In this story, Jesus observes a poor widow put two copper coins into the temple treasury. The difference between her and the wealthy, who presumably give bigger gifts, is that she gives all that she has to live on. While this action is often praised by those who play off heaven and earth, it is noteworthy that in the following passage Jesus predicts the destruction of the temple, which "was adorned with beautiful stones and gifts dedicated to God" (Luke 21:5-6). Having just been told that this wealth derives from donations of people like the poor widow, who reminds us of all the poor who have given beyond what they can afford, the tension cannot be overlooked.

Rather than being an example for sacrificing her livelihood to religion, the widow might be an example for the trouble with religion—linked also to those who "devour widows' houses," mentioned just before this passage (Luke 20:47). Miguel A. De La Torre has a point when he concludes: "The widow requires liberation from the unjust religious structures that rob her of the little she possesses and from her colonized mind."[20] What kind of God would demand that people give up what they need to live a decent life? Is this the true God or the false one—which one is the God of Jesus and which one the god of Caesar?

Another tension between the true God and the false god appears when it comes to the other end of the economic spectrum, the wealthy. While churches are often quick to affirm the wealthy and guarantee them a place in heaven (easy enough if religion is an otherworldly phenomenon), Jesus takes a different approach. Following in the footsteps of his mother, who praises God for lifting up the lowly and pushing the powerful from their thrones, and for filling the hungry with good things while sending the rich away empty (Luke 1:46-55), Jesus talks about wealth where it hurts.

He advises a rich young man to sell what he has, give it to the poor, and thus acquire a treasure in heaven (Mark 10:21)—now explicitly connecting treasures in heaven with giving to the poor. Shortly thereafter he notes that "it is easier for a camel to go through the eye of a needle than for someone who is rich to enter the kingdom of God" (Mark 10:25). While preachers have often tried to water down the challenge—explaining that there might have been a small city gate in Jerusalem called the "needle's eye" so that being saved remains an option for the rich if they make an extra effort—Jesus notes that it is indeed impossible for a rich person to be saved (Mark 10:27). That he also adds the hopeful note that all things are possible for God (Mark 10:27) does not defuse the challenge. Might being "sent away empty" once in a while be part of the process of salvation, like being pushed down from one's throne (Luke 1:52-53)? In any case, with Jesus religion stays squarely rooted in the material realm, and so does the true God. The false god is the one with the quick answers and easy solutions.

One last example for the ongoing struggle between the true God and the false god is the Roman cross on which Jesus is put to death. Christianity contains many different interpretations of the cross, beginning with the diversity of the biblical writings, which have coexisted over the centuries. What is lacking in many of these interpretations, however, is a concern for why Jesus was put to death. As a result, it sometimes looks as if God needed or wanted Jesus to die, conjuring up images of an angry, bloodthirsty, or even a petty God. Because these interpretations often get stuck in otherworldly speculation, they miss the real-life tensions between Jesus and Caesar that led to Jesus's crucifixion. To many of these otherworldly interpreters it must have seemed unfathomable that a supposedly meek and gentle Jesus was crucified; as a result, they made up some scapegoats, for instance by putting the blame on "the Jews."

Yet even the Gospels, which often take great care not to antagonize the Romans, note the real-life tensions. Early on in the Gospel of Mark, when Jesus heals a man on the Sabbath, the religious and political powerbrokers at the scene (identified as "Pharisees" and "Herodians" [Mark 3:6]) conspire to kill him. The method of Jesus's execution is also noteworthy, as there would have been other options: crucifixion was reserved for political insurgents in the Roman Empire. Crucifixions were not rare events, and even mass crucifixions were part of life under the conditions of the empire, calculated to produce collective trauma among the subjects of the empire that, as we know today, can last for generations. Crucifying Jesus would, therefore, send a distinct message of which Paul was still fully aware a few decades later when he preached "Christ crucified" (1 Cor 1:23).

Two things are important here: The first is that the cross shows us the real-life consequences of the way of Jesus over against the way of Caesar—consequences that are suffered to this day by many people.[21] Jesus's experience of brutal pushback is part of the Christian experience. Without romanticizing pushback, experiencing pushback can often help us gauge whether we are following Jesus or Caesar, and whether our religion and our spirituality are material enough. Otherwordly religions and spirituality rarely provoke massive pushback. Second, as Richard Horsley has pointed out, the cross turns out not to be a defeat but provides a source of energy for resistance that, like trauma, can also endure for generations.[22]

> The cross turns out not to be a defeat but provides a source of energy for resistance that, like trauma, can endure for generations.

Whatever theologies of the cross Christians ultimately embrace—we can leave this open for the moment—we will have to make sure that the cross is more than merely an otherworldly symbol. This has implications for how we envision God: only the false god hovers safely above the cross, untouched, unaffected and cold; the true God is the one who moves through real-life suffering and death, deeply affected by it and transforming it.[23]

Similar reflections apply to the resurrection as well. If the resurrection is merely an otherworldly event that is disconnected from Jesus's gruesome struggles with the empire, it likely amounts to nothing more than pie in the sky. If, however, the hope for the resurrection and for life after death is rooted in life before death—continuing the way of Jesus—then it rests on a more solid foundation. Remember, the question whether there is life after death can only be meaningfully addressed in light of the question whether there is life before death! Only the false god promises life after death without attention to life before death.

RIGHT GOD: "GIVE US THIS DAY OUR DAILY BREAD"

The second petition of the Lord's Prayer reads: "Give us this day our daily bread" (Matt 6:11). This seems a simple request, especially when made by those who take for granted that they are fed every day. For those who are fed, another word from Jesus might be more relevant than the petition for bread: "One does not live by bread alone but by every word that comes from the mouth of God" (Matt 4:4). This is Jesus's response to the temptation of the devil to turn stones into bread. Yet even that statement is based on the recognition that bread remains necessary for life. Jesus does not support the common religious efforts of separating the material and the spiritual, playing off earth and heaven.

Moreover, we should not assume that bread and the word of God can be divided according to what is commonly considered material and spiritual. In the Jewish tradition in which Jesus is immersed, God's word is spiritual and material at the same time. At one point the word of God is likened to "a hammer that breaks a rock in pieces" (Jer 23:29). And even when Jesus is famished and yearns for bread, like for example in the temptation stories in Matthew and Luke, he never forgets the life-sustaining material qualities of the word of God (Matt 4:4; Luke 4:4).

Just as the word is not just a spiritual matter, bread is not merely a material matter. Bread, like the word, sustains the whole person and symbolizes what the empire can give or withhold in order to manipulate people all the way to the core, including their spiritualities. For good reasons, the Roman Empire promoted *panem et circenses* "bread and games," which in combination helped shore up its power. In addition, bread also symbolizes the spiritualities that are linked with the hard work of peasant communities and communal production. This brings us back to the tension between Jesus and Caesar: while Caesar uses bread in order to pacify people, Jesus returns our gaze to the broader picture, which includes the experience of the lack of bread but also the production of bread. First-century peasant communities would have been able to relate to this—as would twenty-first-century communities of working people.

Today, a closer look at what is too quickly condemned as "materialism" holds similar insights. As pointed out above, a cell phone may be a material possession but its importance is much more profound. For many people, it provides an essential link to others: "Can you hear me now?" was a brilliant advertising campaign by Verizon because a cell phone is a way of making oneself heard. Cell phones are of particular importance in areas around the globe that do not have a strong infrastructure of conduits and wires. What is considered material and spiritual is closely connected by many bonds.

Thinking about God in these terms fundamentally transforms what many assume religion to be. The Christian tradition and ties to the faith of Israel, in particular, bring together the material and the spiritual in powerful ways. Over time, whenever Christianity forgot about these ties, a reduction of religion to otherworldly spirituality was often the result.[24] Even Jesus's titles of *Lord* and *Savior* have strong material connotations, as we have seen, since they subvert Caesar's political power and his ways of providing for the livelihood of his people. In this way, even the theology of the Apostle Paul who uses these titles—falsely considered otherworldly[25]—highlights the holistic reality of Jesus.

The miracles of Jesus also offer key examples for how material and spiritual matters always belong together. Healing and forgiveness of sins go hand in hand in Jesus's ministry. One of the first healings of Jesus in the Gospel of Mark combines the two, beginning with the forgiveness of sins, which raises some eyebrows because only God can forgive sins. Jesus's response poses a conundrum: "Which is easier, to say to the paralytic,

'Your sins are forgiven,' or to say, 'Stand up and take your mat and walk'?"
(Mark 2:9). In response, he heals the person with paralysis whose sins he
had forgiven and who now takes his bed and walks away; the healing rein-
forces his authority to forgive sins (Mark 2:10-12).

The combination of healing and forgiveness not only underscores the
combination of material and spiritual, it also embeds Jesus's miracles into
the broader context of politics, economics, and culture. Healing and forgiveness reestablish people's place in the community and in the world. In
some of Jesus's exorcisms a similar dynamic is at work: driving out a band
of demons called "legion," Jesus challenges the powers of the empire (a
legion was, of course, a unit of the Roman army) and restores power to the
community (Mark 5:1-20).[26]

In the Gospels, miracles are interpreted as acts of power (Greek: *dyna-
meis*) rather than as acts of magic that are based on a distinction between
natural and supernatural. In other words, the power of Jesus's miracles is
not directed at transgressing the limits of what modern people might consider the natural, but at showing the power of God in resistance to evil and
sin that was considered insurmountable.[27] In Jesus's ministry, miracles are
directed at whatever it is that keeps people down, including the Roman
occupation and the political and economic pressures of the day. In this
regard, bringing good news to the poor—the conclusion of Jesus's pro-
grammatic statement in Matt 11:4-5—may well be the greatest miracle
of all; is that not the miracle that people even today are likely to find the
hardest to believe, even more so than raising the dead? What is easier to
accomplish, the forgiveness of sins, the healing of the sick, the raising of a
few dead people, or that the masses of the poor will no longer be poor? In
Jesus's ministry, these things cannot easily be separated.

The power of Jesus's miracles is not directed
at transgressing the limits of what modern
people might consider the natural, but at
showing the power of God in resistance
to evil and sin that was considered
insurmountable.

A final example of the separation of material and spiritual is the separation of the immanent and the transcendent. Some liberal Christians have given focus primarily to the immanent, in reaction to a widespread Christian fixation on what is considered transcendent. The problem is that a focus on what is considered immanent often gets stuck in a particular status quo perspective. Consider the parallel to the Sadducees at the time of Jesus, a group whose theology was also firmly rooted in this world to such a degree that they denied the resurrection of the dead. Some have even caricaturized the Sadducees as the liberals of the ancient world. Some of these denials of transcendence are linked to positions of privilege, which are generally content with the prevailing conditions. If life treats you well, you do not need to rock the boat. If sufficient bread is available, it is not necessary to pose any challenges to dominant immanent reality.

The petition for bread can help us put things in a different frame: if bread is scarce and if immanent reality is letting you down, then there is a need to push beyond it. The peasant population of Jesus's day, the African American slaves of the eighteenth and nineteenth centuries, and many struggling people today know that dominant immanent reality is not enough. For them, transcendent reality is a promise that "another world is possible."[28] But note the direction: the promise is not for some unreachable great beyond—this is not about transcendence without immanence. The promise of transcendence is for an alternative immanent reality and for another way of life, here and now.

> The promise of transcendence is for an alternative immanent reality and for another way of life, here and now. Transcendence continues in the healing work of Jesus, as opposed to the traumatizing work of the Roman Empire.

With Jesus, God's transcendence is not to be found somewhere up in the sky; rather, transcendence starts in the immanence of the manger in Bethlehem, as opposed to the thrones in Jerusalem and Rome.[29] And transcendence continues in the healing work of Jesus, as opposed to the traumatizing work of the Roman Empire.

CONCLUSION: LOVE, TOUGH AND DOWN TO EARTH

Concluding that the concern for the material and the spiritual comes together in love, the kind of love that is embodied by Jesus, sounds like an uncontroversial and safe statement to make. Yet keep in mind what this sort of love meant in the village communities where Jesus was at work: it included political and economic practices like the sharing of power, of bread, and of other resources, and it led to the cancellation of debt, which we will address in the next chapter.[30]

Moreover, love is not having warm feelings for others but is manifest in whatever is life-giving. In the confrontation with Caesar, love takes on what we might call the form of "tough love," a down-to-earth love that that pushes back against whatever is death-dealing. This is best seen in Jesus's ongoing struggles with the powers that be, challenging the self-centeredness of the religious leaders (those Pharisees who are "hypocrites" [Matt 23:1-36]) and the political and economic leaders (Herod "that fox" in Luke 13:32 and the royals "dressed in soft robes" in Matt 11:8), which leads to the pushback that eventually results in Jesus's execution as a political rebel.

The best summary of this comprehensive perspective can be found in the so-called double commandment to love God and one's neighbors as oneself (Mark 12:29-31). Jesus puts two commandments together that are usually not found in close proximity, giving us a comprehensive perspective.[31] There is no need to split up these loves of God and neighbor so that one is material and the other spiritual, or that one is immanent and the other transcendent. Love of neighbor can be deeply spiritual if we understand our connectedness as human beings, and love of God can be deeply material if we understand that the things of God can never be limited to another world because God is the creator of this world. In either case, this love is down-to-earth.

In this down-to-earth love, Jesus embodies our relatedness to God and to each other in all directions, transforming both the material and the spiritual forever.

QUESTIONS FOR REFLECTION AND DISCUSSION

1. What are some examples of how Christians have neglected the material world?

2. Collect some examples for how Christians have taken the material world seriously.

3. Where are the growing edges in your community in regard to love that is tough and down to earth?

Chapter 4
GOD VS. MAMMON

On Religion and Economics

Failure to understand the tension between life-giving and malignant religion has seduced many into blindly supporting economic systems that benefit elite minorities and relegate the vast majority of humanity and the planet to exploitation and suffering. The matter of economics is a crucial topic in our exploration of the ongoing tensions between Jesus and Caesar: Of the thirty-one parables in the Synoptic Gospels, more than half (nineteen) reflect directly on class, inequality, worker pay, indebtedness, the misuse of wealth, and the distribution of wealth!

Whatever statistics are being used, it is widely acknowledged that the differentials between rich and poor are still growing today, despite continued hopes that a rising tide would eventually lift all boats. As mentioned earlier, in the Roman Empire in the year 150 CE the top 1 percent controlled merely 16 percent of all wealth, while today in the United States 1 percent control more than 40 percent of all wealth.[1] Moreover, in the year 2017, only eight individuals owned as much wealth as half of humanity, 3.3 billion people, combined. In the year 2001, two hundred twenty-five individuals were in that position.[2]

At the same time, in the United States 43 percent of all children live below or near the poverty line, and many of them are what the government calls "food insecure," which means that they sometimes go to bed

73

hungry.[3] With national unemployment rates below 5 percent, it is easy to see that most of their parents must be working, without being able to make ends meet. If the divine judgment is tied to how the rest of us do or do not relate to the least of these, as Jesus states in Matthew 25:40 and 25:45, we are not dealing merely with a social problem here but with a deeply theological and spiritual issue.

The tensions between Jesus and Caesar get deeper under our skin when they include not only politics but also economics. While there is concern that religion and politics have entered into relationships that are too close, we should be even more concerned about the relation between religion and economics. Fortunately, many Americans still have a fairly healthy suspicion of politics, even though they oddly suspend it sometimes when their favorite candidate or party is in charge. However, many Americans have a fairly low level of suspicion when it comes to economics. Common political critiques of big government are not necessarily matched by economic critiques of big corporations, with the possible exception of criticism of CEO pay rates. In other words, as much as Americans question political structures they tend to go softer on economic ones.

Moreover, while in the United States there is the stated principle of the separation of church and state, there is no comparable principle of the separation of church and economy. As a result, dominant religion and dominant economics are entangled even more than dominant religion and dominant politics. Not surprisingly, American Christianity has become one of the pillars of neoliberal capitalism where power is increasingly in the hands of the few,[4] which has been promoted in the United States since the 1980s. What does it say that many Christians can imagine the end of the world but not the end of capitalism, and where does that leave us in the struggle of Jesus vs. Caesar?

The good news is that, despite these entanglements, many faith communities share concerns for poverty and the poor, embodying a core concern of Jesus. So, how might a deeper understanding of Jesus vs. Caesar help us develop these concerns further? Reflecting on relationships is a first step: poor people do not exist in isolation from the wealthy—although this is often assumed, leading people to blame the poor for their misfortune. How are poor people related to the rest of the community and to society?

In Jesus's time, these connections were more openly visible: in the wider Roman Empire, wealth was derived from the collection of taxes and interest from the population, which was often pushed into poverty by this very system. Even today, poverty still tends to be produced in relation to wealth: debt continues to be a problem, but exorbitant taxes have been replaced by low wages and income. When we talk about poverty, therefore, we also need to talk about wealth—talk about poverty without talking about wealth is profoundly misleading.[5] In this sense, it would be better to talk about impoverished people rather than poor people.

Wealth in Jesus's time was also derived from the patronage system, which established relationships between the wealthiest and the rest of society. Caesar was at the top of this patronage system, embodying both supreme power and supreme wealth. Jesus, as we will see, did not have the luxury of operating outside of this system: he had to establish his own stand within it and against it, and move from there.

Today, although there is no officially sanctioned patronage system, networks of patronage continue to exist. Campaign funding and the practice of lobbying are examples of how patronage functions in politics—even if these are only the tips of the iceberg—and the business community has its own networks and associated perks. What is less openly discussed is that many well-to-do churches and religious communities function in the same way. Like Jesus, pastors and churches do not have the luxury of operating outside of this system. Where do we take our stand and how will we move?

THE CONFLICT OF ECONOMICS: NOT WHAT WE THOUGHT

When we begin to understand that economics and faith cannot be separated, we are forced to take another look at how the relationship between the two shapes up.[6] In the Galilee of Jesus's time, Roman power was at work indirectly through client kings like Herod Antipas, who imposed tributes on the communities, which had to be paid on top of regular taxes. The burdens of this system were so heavy that people often had to go into debt, and when they could no longer service their debt, they were forced to become sharecroppers on their own land. Others were pushed off their land completely and driven into the emerging cities where they worked in service and large Roman construction projects. Jesus himself grew up in a family of landless day-laboring construction workers.

The patronage system established another kind of relationship, which tied together patrons and clients from the ruling class, politicians, and others who had some power and prominence. The Roman emperors themselves established patron-client relationships with elites around the empire by distributing offices, honors, and favors. A good emperor was seen as a benefactor and caring patriarch. Such patronage continued on many levels. In Judea, patronage also characterized the relationship between Herod (Herod Antipas's father) and the priesthood of the temple in Jerusalem at the time of Jesus's birth.

The flow of money in these relationships thus determined the kind of power that was wielded, and it shaped religious developments. In return for the patronage of the Roman emperor under Herod, for instance, the Jewish priests in the temple in Jerusalem performed sacrifices in honor of Rome and Caesar (though there were no sacrifices to Rome and Caesar directly), and the Roman eagle was displayed above the gates of the temple. In Galilee, on the other hand, farther away from direct Roman rule (and benefiting less from its patronage), there would have been a slightly different spirit, which was more open to welcoming Jesus over Caesar.

This is the context for one of the most well-known, but perhaps also the most ignored, sayings of Jesus, namely that it is not possible to serve both God and mammon. While the language of mammon is perhaps more familiar, the NRSV translation uses the term *wealth* instead: "No one can serve two masters; for a slave will either hate the one and love the other, or be devoted to the one and despise the other. You cannot serve God and wealth" (Matt 6:24). What is remarkable about this statement is that wealth is discussed at the level of God. In other words, wealth is not just a matter of morality and ethics; it is a matter of theology. The question is whom people worship and to whom they devote themselves: God or wealth. The struggle between Jesus and Caesar here turns into the struggle between God and wealth.

> Wealth is not just a matter of morality and ethics, it is a matter of theology. The question is whom people worship and to whom they devote themselves: God or wealth.

In the patronage system there was always the danger that patrons claimed too much power over their clients; here, we are talking about an extreme situation where the wealthy patron takes the place of God. For the peasants who owed tribute and taxes the temptation to give devotion to the wealthy might have been limited, as they would have harbored a good deal of resentment. Yet, as they were under tremendous pressure, it must have often looked to them as if they had no choice than to serve those whom they owed tribute and taxes.

If wealth taking the place of God was a problem in the time of Jesus,[7] the problem has only gotten worse today. Under the conditions of neoliberal capitalism, money often takes on a life of its own, as financial markets depend on speculation as much as on performance indicators. In addition, money factors into decisions made in the world of business, more so than actual products or the welfare of workers. CEOs are charged with increasing the value of the stock of their companies; attention to workers and to products must be subordinated to this goal. Thus, it could be said that a corporation like the Ford Motor Company is in the business of making money rather than cars, or that the production of cars is subordinated to the production of money. CEOs and the leadership of a given company have little choice in this matter, as they are bound by a legal precedent.[8]

This economic situation presents us with a fundamental theological challenge today. This is not just about the ethics of wealth and what people end up doing with their wealth. The question is to whom we devote

ourselves and whom we worship, and who gets left out. Ethical consider-
ations are not unimportant, of course, but they follow from our theological commitments: Are we devoting ourselves to Jesus (and the people he
cared about) or to Caesar. Are we worshiping God or money?

At the heart of Christianity is, therefore, a decision. Evangelical Christianity had that right all along: confronted with the tension between Jesus
and Caesar, a personal decision for Jesus needs to be made. Neutrality is
not an option because it amounts to going with the dominant flow—devotion to Caesar and the worship of money. Now we see more clearly
what this decision implies, both positively and negatively. The key question of Jesus to his disciples and, by extension, to us is not whether they
have faith or not, but in what exactly they believe ("Who do you say that
I am?" Mark 8:29). The decision for Jesus has consequences, as it is also
a decision against something else. Making a decision for Jesus means, at
the same time, to make a decision against Caesar. Saying that Jesus is Lord
implies that Caesar is not. In a next step, this decision turns into a decision for God and against money.

But who would devote themselves to money and wealth and worship
it? It is easy enough to point to Caesar, Herod, and the superrich. But perhaps Jesus's challenge hits more closely to home than most people realize.
In a world that is built on trust in its basic economic structures, we must
indeed ask ourselves in what and whom we trust, in the strongest sense
of the word. Current investments and retirement plans, for instance, are
built on trust not only that the money we invest will be available when we
need it but also that this money keeps growing, despite occasional (and
increasingly severe) economic downturns. Both in the days of Caesar and
today, wealth is ultimately a matter of maintaining a close relationship
with the powers that be and the trust that these relationships will last.

> Both in the days of Caesar and today, wealth
> is ultimately a matter of maintaining a close
> relationship with the powers that be and
> the trust that these relationships will last.

In the Roman Empire, wealth was maintained by the trust established between patrons and clients, while it was produced by tributes and taxation. Wealth was not just there, it had to be created by the communities from whom it could be extracted in order to be reinvested in patron-client relations. In contemporary capitalism it is assumed that wealth is maintained and grows via the stock market and the aptly named "trust funds," but here, too, a great deal of wealth continues to be produced by people whose work contributes to making the wealthy wealthier.

The pursuit of this kind of wealth follows the logic of Caesar, which continues to make the rich richer, then as now. Jesus, it seems, follows a different logic. The wealth of the rich he assumes—as do most of his listeners, or some of his parables would not work—is "dishonest" (Luke 16:8-10). To be sure, there is still some use even for questionable wealth: in the parable of the dishonest manager, Jesus advises to use this dishonest wealth to make friends, that is, to build solidarity among the people (Luke 16:9). In the story of the rich young man, Jesus suggests giving his wealth to the poor because it is hard "for those who have wealth to enter the kingdom of God"—"for mortals it is impossible, but not for God" (Mark 10:17-27).

Jesus pulls the false god of wealth from his throne and reminds us of the true God. This move creates space for what amounts to alternative economic relationships that take the common people seriously. In these relationships, working people play a role that fundamentally differs from the dominant economics of Caesar. While for the Greeks and their Roman admirers labor was valued less than other pursuits, Jesus kept close to working people all his life. Some of this shows through in a little comment in the Gospel of John: "My father is still working, and I am also working" (John 5:17).

In the Pauline literature the value of work in the divine economy is addressed in the often-recited statement that "anyone unwilling to work should not eat" (2 Thess 3:10). While this statement has, unfortunately, often been used against working people—blaming the underemployed and the unemployed in particular—there is also a sense in which it honors workers. Keep in mind who, from the perspective of working people like Jesus and Paul, does not value work and who is usually unwilling to work: the privileged, like Caesar and his wealthy patron friends, including the proverbial 1 percent today, as the bulk of their wealth derives from the work of others, whose wages and benefits they depress for even more gain.

WRONG GOD: WHAT DIFFERENCE DOES IT MAKE?

Prophetic critiques of exploitation and forced labor are well known. Examples include Jeremiah 22:13: "Woe to him who builds his house by unrighteousness, and his upper rooms by injustice; who makes his neighbors work for nothing, and does not give them their wages."[9] Jesus agrees that "a laborer deserves to be paid" (Luke 10:7), and there is a good chance that he experienced unfair labor practices and perhaps even unemployment when growing up as a construction worker. One of the biggest construction projects in Galilee during Jesus's life (twenty miles from Nazareth) was the city of Tiberias, on the western shore of Lake Galilee, named in honor of the Roman emperor Tiberius. Founded by Herod Antipas in 20 CE, considerable construction was going on there.

What is behind this ongoing abuse of workers? Construction workers (immigrants in our own time, displaced peasants in Jesus's time) are often treated as dispensable, and today, wage theft has become an epidemic.[10] Once again, we are dealing with more than an ethical problem. At stake is nothing less than people's relationship with God. In Isaiah, the people ask God: "'Why do we fast, but you do not see? Why humble ourselves, but you do not notice?'" and God answers: "Look, you serve your own interest on your fast day, and oppress all your workers" (Isaiah 58:3). According to Isaiah, only when these problems are corrected can people experience God's guidance (Isaiah 58:11). Worshiping the wrong god, choosing wealth—gained by oppressing workers then and now—over God and over people, is more than just an ethical problem.

Contemporary economists argue that economics does not have to be a zero-sum game: when the rich are getting richer the poor do not necessarily have to be getting poorer. In fact, contemporary economics assumes that when the rich are getting richer all are better off, as "a rising tide lifts all boats."[11] Some argue that there is a difference between ancient times and to-day. At the time of Jesus, they grant, economics may have been a zero-sum game, where wealth was produced on the back of others. The difference today, they assume, is financial capital, which produces wealth seemingly without labor.[12] In this case, there may no longer be a conflict between the interests of Jesus and Caesar, or between God and wealth.

The contemporary god of wealth apparently wants what everyone wants: raising people out of poverty by producing more wealth. Of course, this god of wealth demands trust: without faith that capitalism works and is here to stay, things would collapse. The financial transactions of the wealthy are based on such trust that the god of wealth will provide; everyone else is expected to comply and make sacrifices to that god, even if there are no immediate benefits.[13] Threatening and questioning this trust that wealth will benefit everyone are economic regulations and the labor movement, and this is one reason why both regulations and organized labor have been severely attacked in recent years.

Yet the age-old suspicion that wealth is presenting us with trust in a false god cannot be set aside so easily. The petition for daily bread in the Lord's Prayer reminds us that bread is lacking for a lot of people. This is not just the case in Jesus's Galilee, where peasants and workers found themselves under pressure. In the contemporary United States, poverty is rampant, and more than a third of all children are growing up below the poverty line, as mentioned above. From the perspective of many of the so-called "working poor," the hope that a rising tide will lift all boats is not just an illusion—it amounts to heresy and idolatry, that is, the worship of a false god that is at the heart of malignant faith.[14]

Why is there no bread for all, even during times of great economic booms, when the rising tide supposedly lifts all? A common response is that people are lazy. Too often, this accusation is internalized even by those who lack the necessities of life for their families, and who thus blame themselves. Yet when most poor people in the United States are working—often more than just one job—how can they be accused of laziness?

This makes no sense, but when logic fails, the logic of wealth kicks in, seeing lack of wealth as lack of divine blessing. Yet this logic of wealth amounts to the logic of a false god, as the prophets and Jesus knew.

Providing charitable support for the many who live in or near poverty—their numbers are at 50 percent or higher, both today and at the time of Jesus[15]—may seem the right thing to do, but charity produces two other problems. The first one is that charity and handouts are only stopgap measures that do not address the deeper problem. The second, bringing us back to the tension between Jesus and Caesar, is that charity and handouts do not call into question the false god of wealth—in fact, charity and handouts protect this god since they allow unjust relationships to continue. In other words, churches whose ministries are exclusively charity-based are in danger of contributing to the worship of the false god of wealth!

> Churches whose ministries are exclusively charity-based are in danger of contributing to the worship of the false god of wealth!

Following the wrong god has consequences also for human relationships. Based on what we have found so far, the Roman Empire shaped relationships in two steps: On the one hand, it divided the people and thus conquered; on the other hand, it also managed to unify and conquer. Divide-and-conquer is a time-honored method of social control. In the time of Jesus, the Jewish population was divided into people who benefited from the status quo and those who did not. Jewish tax collectors, for instance, benefited from the system of taxation, while Jewish peasants and workers did not. Religious officials that were included into the patronage system benefited from imperial wealth and power, while other religious officials did not. The dividing line in this case was not between Jews and Romans but between Jews and other Jews, which may explain some of Jesus's harsh words against Jews in the Gospel of John.[16] This strategy continues today when workers are divided according to the lines of race, gender, or sexuality; both management and labor relations experts (sometimes called union busters) have been known to make use of it.[17]

On the other hand, we should not forget how the Roman Empire also unified in order to conquer. Patron-client relationships brought people together who did not have a common religion, ethnicity, or geographical location. This is how the Roman emperor built relationships among the elites and among those who felt they were sharing in the interests of the ruling class. Jewish tax collectors in Palestine, for instance, might have seen their interests more in alignment with the Roman emperor and his client kings rather than with fellow Jews who worked in the fields or in construction. This unify-and-conquer strategy is found today also in certain forms of racism, where white people are primed to feel that they have more in common with other white people than with racial minorities. Such racism covers up the fact that, for the most part, white workers have more in common with black workers than with their white employers.

This might throw some light on Jesus's enigmatic sayings that he would bring not peace but a sword that have long troubled good mainline Christians. According to the Gospel of Matthew (10:34-36), the tension goes from the bottom up (in contrast to Luke 12:51-53): sons rebel against fathers, daughters against mothers. While divisions and tensions are usually seen as problematic by people of faith, this rebellion may be a way of fighting false unity in order to arrive at more appropriate forms of unity. Klaus Wengst observes that Jesus "does not lament over this division from below; that is exactly what he wants."[18] The good news, we should add, is that those divisions allow for a new and deeper kind of solidarity.[19]

WRONG GOD, RIGHT GOD: THE STRUGGLE CONTINUES

While those who are benefiting from empire and the ripple effect of economic bubbles may take for granted the identity of God and wealth—or of Jesus and Caesar—those on whose back the empire or the bubble economies have been built have always had their doubts. Working people often bring other perspectives to the table, and holders of dominant power and wealth are constantly worried about what might happen when these perspectives are amplified and come out into the open. Jesus drawing a firm line between God and wealth is just one example of what happens when perspectives of working people—who are not the minority but the majority of a population—break through.

The parable of the workers in the vineyard in the Gospel of Matthew (Matt 20:1-16) illustrates what is at stake. In this parable workers are hired at various times during the day, with the last ones working only an hour. At the end of the day the owner of the vineyard pays each worker "a denarion," the usual daily wage (20:9). No doubt, this parable pushes against the logic of wealth that dictates that everyone is rewarded according to what they contribute—a logic that in the parable is demanded even by those workers who worked the longest on that day (20:12).

The tension between God and wealth, or between Jesus and Caesar, that plays itself out here seems simple. The logic of wealth demands fairness, the logic of God is "generous" (20:15). Yet this interpretation does not take into account some of the deeper tensions. The workers who only work one hour do not do so because they are lazy; they do so because they could not find employment (20:7), which is a common experience for workers all over the world. Even capitalism, in order to function properly, requires a certain minimum of unemployment, as experts remind us.[20] Nevertheless, in order to survive, all need some income. This is what the landowner in the parable provides, with Jesus adding that "the last will be first, and the first will be last" (20:16).

It would be easy to spiritualize the whole episode and to talk about God's grace as opposed to Caesar's works-righteousness. But this parable also speaks to a deep-seated struggle between the true God and a false god. Unlike the false god, the true God whom Jesus represents counters a system that works against people: day laborers who do not receive their wages may have to send their children to bed hungry, while landowners are more likely to have some reserves (however limited they might be, especially in the world of small businesses).

Looking at things from the perspective of working people should not be too hard, as 99 percent of us have to work for a living. Workers at the bottom of the system are always hit harder, if their wages are not stolen altogether. Miguel A. De La Torre reflects on the reality of day laborers today: "How many day laborers end up working all day only to be paid a fraction of their worth because they have no recourse?"[21] This is not just a moral question—it is a theological one and it helps us get a better sense of the struggle of Jesus vs. Caesar and the implications for us.

But even for those whose wages are still more adequate, the logic of wealth as it currently functions imposes downward pressures. Stagnating wages, loss of benefits, loss of job security or seniority, and so on, are widely experienced even by the middle class, while those closer to the top who are considered more valuable continue to enjoy raises, bonuses, and benefits. This situation resembles indeed a zero-sum game, as the fortunes of the 1 percent continue to grow while those of the 99 percent stagnate or decline. Those who do the math for themselves and their loved ones should not forget to adjust for inflation and keep in mind what the next recession might do to their futures.

Jesus embraces the tradition and message of the Hebrew prophets: wealth built on the backs of others is problematic, and today more so than ever as the gap between the top and the bottom continues to widen. While for almost five decades liberation theologies have developed these insights further, even mainline churches have begun to recognize and address these problems. In its current Social Principles, The United Methodist Church states: "We support measures that would reduce the concentration of wealth in the hands of a few."[22]

What about the wealthy 1 percent? Are they excluded from following Jesus? In the Gospel of Luke, there is a reference to several prominent and wealthy women who were on the road with the Jesus movement (Luke 8:3). Another example is Zacchaeus, who gives half of his possessions to the poor and promises to return fourfold to those he has defrauded (Luke 19:8), thus decolonizing not only his economic relationships but also his mind and his relationship to God.[23] The wealthy are challenged but not excluded from following Jesus, it seems, unless they exclude themselves. The challenge amounts to an invitation to follow the true God and renounce the false one.

Clearly, the tensions between Jesus and Caesar continue, even though theology has often tried to explain away conflicts and tensions. One time-honored way of explaining away conflicts and tensions between Jesus and Caesar is blaming the victims. This happens frequently when people are not able to make ends meet. Ancient examples include the effort of Job's friends to find explanations for Job's suffering—a person who loses everything without being at fault—in order to normalize the situation and make an otherwise unbearable situation bearable. Yet Job bears witness to the fact that blaming the victims in the face of their suffering is not the best way forward, as it maintains an unbearable status quo that crushes them.[24] In the Gospel of John, the disciples wonder what caused the condition of a man who was born blind: did he sin or did his parents sin? Jesus categorically refuses to blame either the victim or his family. He then proceeds to heal the man (John 9:1-12) without explaining away the tensions.

Where do people get the idea that victims should be blamed for their own misfortune? The logic of wealth is part of the problem, lifting up those who have gained wealth and pushing down those without wealth. Blaming the victims is part of the struggle between Jesus and Caesar, yet such efforts break down as soon as we take a deeper look at what is happening to large numbers of people in real life.[25]

The real struggle between Jesus and Caesar is, thus, not primarily between individuals, some of which are doing better for themselves than others. The real struggle is embodied in communities that are held down by the false god of money and power (Caesar) and that stand to benefit from the true God. This is not a struggle between a minority of marginalized communities against the majority of the population, as we often assume today. The reverse is the case: this is a struggle between a minority of those who hold wealth and power and the majority of humanity and the planet. This majority, sometimes called the 99 percent, consists of those who are experiencing the pressures of the system in one way or another. This majority includes even middle-class communities in the United States, as they are only a few paychecks away from bankruptcy, their jobs and futures (think retirement plans) are less and less secure, and where children can no longer assume that they will do as well or better than their parents.

In recent Jesus research, Richard Horsley draws attention to the fact that Jesus was organizing communities, his mission "focused not on individuals but on people involved in families and village communities."[26] These social forms were disintegrating not of their own fault but because of the actions of an empire that tore communities apart by destroying their resources and their spirit. In this context, Jesus's blessings and curses, as narrated in the Sermon on the Plain (Luke 6), turn things upside down. Communities who likely blamed themselves for their misfortune (or who were blamed by the spirit of the empire), are declared blessed: "blessed are you who are poor...hungry...weep"; while those who considered themselves blessed are declared cursed: "woe to you who are rich...full...laughing" (Luke 6:20-25). All of this points away from the false god and toward the true God who backs up these blessings and curses.

Right God: "And Forgive Us Our Debts"

The third petition of the Lord's Prayer (Matt 6:12) reads: "And forgive us our debts, as we also have forgiven our debtors," following the petition for daily bread. Both requests deal with material realities in the life of the people at the time of Jesus. Debt, in this context, is not primarily a religious matter but has to do with the actual financial indebtedness of some to others. Concern for the forgiveness of debt also links Jesus to the tradition of the Jubilee Year in Leviticus, according to which debt forgiveness was practiced after every forty-nine years.[27] While some scholars feel that such debt forgiveness may have never been practiced, due to the scarcity of historical data it is hard to rule it out. Scholarly doubt in this case may have more to do with a theological judgment about what faith in God can and cannot accomplish.

During Jesus's life, large parts of the population felt the pressures of an empire that demanded not only the payment of tributes and taxes but also the servicing of debt. Such debt was incurred when the productivity

87

of land and labor was not sufficient to sustain life due to the increasing demands of the empire. Indebtedness to the empire and the lack of bread are, thus, closely related. And, like the lack of bread, debt is hardly the fault of most of the people who incur it. In this sense, the notion of debt is the opposite of the notion of guilt (and related notions of feeling guilty) and of the notion of trespassing, which is how the Lord's Prayer is recited by various Christian denominations today. Debt points beyond debtors to that which puts people in debt.

While indebtedness was a serious burden on the contemporaries of Jesus, who were often pushed off their lands by mounting debt, today debt continues to be a burden. Debt is often accrued because people are not able to sustain themselves and their families. In addition, our contemporary credit system lures many people into spending large amounts of money that they are unable to repay, a problem that is amplified by the deliberate production of desire to consume. Unfair lending practices, like payday lending charging exorbitant interest rates to people who have no other access to funds (often single mothers and minorities), make a bad situation worse.

Frequently the root of this kind of debt is substandard wages, including a low minimum wage that makes it increasingly impossible for people to feed their families. Debt, labor, and wealth are thus closely related. Praying for debt relief, therefore, means praying for a world where debt no longer crushes communities and—equally important—committing oneself to forgiving the debt of others as one is able. Forgiveness of debt, thus, becomes a matter of deep solidarity that runs counter to Caesar's strategy of divide, conquer, and collect.

> Forgiveness of debt, thus, becomes a matter of deep solidarity that runs counter to Caesar's strategy of divide, conquer, and collect.

Jesus's parable of the unforgiving servant demonstrates how the true God is at work, beginning with the solidarity of working people. This parable tells the story of a service worker who is unwilling to forgive another worker (Matt 18:23-35). In this tale a very unusual employer—certainly not Caesar—forgives some worker an enormous amount of debt. This act of the forgiveness of debt means that the worker now has some options that he did not have before. When a coworker approaches him about the forgiveness of a much smaller debt, this worker is now free to forgive the debt—an action that he possibly could not have afforded before. In the parable, the worker nevertheless chooses to collect the debt rather than forgive it. Since the fellow worker is unable to pay, he has him thrown in prison, following the logic of credit, wealth, and money.

There is, however, another pattern present here, one that follows the logic of those who are not in control. Following this logic, which seems to be the way of Jesus, the better choice would be to forgive the debt of the fellow worker. The reasoning is simple, but it only works when we see through the false promises of the logic of wealth: the refusal to forgive a fellow worker's debt results in every worker having to fight on his or her own. The worker who collected the small debt gains a small amount of money but loses something much more valuable, namely solidarity. Forgiving debt would deepen solidarity among workers and establish relationships that reinforce a community where people support each other and help each other out when they are in need.

Here is where it makes sense to mention Jesus's often misunderstood commandment to love one's enemies. As Horsley has pointed out, this love counters the divide-and-conquer strategy of the empire, especially when it is seen in the context of the village communities where the logic of wealth has introduced divisions and competition.[28] Wengst also agrees that love for enemies finds its location in the disputes among the lower classes.[29] Enemy love is not some romantic ideal ("be nice to Caesar and his representatives") but what helps overcome shortsighted divisions among the villages and between working people.

Read this way, the forgiveness of debt, according to the logic of Jesus, means deepening bonds of solidarity among people that work together for the common good and nurturing shared power able to sustain it. To return to the parable: if the employer were to change his mind at some point in the future and chalk up debt again, the solidarity of the workers is the only thing that counts, as money is quickly spent and gone. The logic of Jesus that shines through here is a logic of solidarity, grounded in organizing workers and the community.[30]

Interestingly enough, in the parable of the unforgiving servant, the worker whose debt is forgiven is the only one who does not seem to realize what is going on. The other workers understand what is happening and protest his actions (Matt 18:31). Working people who have long experienced a shared powerlessness may have a head start in developing a sense for the importance of organizing and solidarity, but all of us can learn.

Once again, at stake is a vision of who God is and who we are in relation to God. Rather than moralizing about what people should or should not do, Jesus's parable of the unforgiving servant simply describes how power flows and what our options are. We can follow the logic of Caesar, or we can follow the logic of Jesus. The decision is not as hard as it might seem. Working people, like the ones in the parable, would not have a hard time grasping which logic is more beneficial to them.

Jesus's logic—the logic of solidarity and of organizing—should therefore not be hard to understand for the 99 percent who have to work for a living, including all who are struggling to flourish under the world order of empire, because it benefits them and it is life-giving to them. The powerful, employers and bankers, on the other hand, may have a more difficult time learning, yet they too are invited to follow the logic of Jesus and to give up the logic of Caesar.

Preachers who think (and preach) from the perspective of Caesar face similar difficulties. Their attempts to moralize about Jesus's parable of the unforgiving servant rarely succeed. The argument goes something like this: someone has forgiven you a great debt, now you are morally required to forgive as well, even if it is not in your best interest. Such moralizing did not work in the Roman Empire or, almost two thousand years later, with the US government bailouts during the Great Recession. The logic of Jesus, which is the logic of grace, on the other hand, provides a different metric for success: when the 99 percent begin to organize, often debt is actually forgiven.[31]

In sum, if debt is one of the greatest tools for maintaining top-down power (then and now), then everything changes when God forgives our debt and if we amplify this move by forgiving the debts of others.

CONCLUSION: PULLED TOGETHER BY GRACE OR APART BY WEALTH

The logic of Caesar, which is the logic of wealth, tends to play people off against each other, making it appear as if inequalities are God-given and natural. The logic of Jesus, on the other hand—the logic of community, organizing, and solidarity—provides alternatives. In the days of Jesus, the flourishing of life depended on whether village communities were able to pull together in solidarity or not. In this struggle, the Jesus movement sometimes found allies in unlikely places, including wealthy women or a group of Pharisees who warn Jesus that Herod wants to have him killed (Luke 8:3; 13:31).

What is more, the logic of community, organizing, and solidarity involves not just people but also God. God's very self in Jesus joins in solidarity with people who are trying to make a living and with them endures the consequences. In the words of Wengst: "In the crucified Jesus God has not allied himself with the great, but on the contrary with those on the periphery."[32] De La Torre echoes this conclusion: "The importance of Jesús' crucifixion is that this is the historical moment when Jesús chose solidarity with the world's marginalized, even unto death."[33] What emerges here is what I have called deep solidarity elsewhere: the kind of community where people pull together without needing to give up or erase their differences. In fact, deep solidarity not only allows for differences but flourishes when people put them to use for the good of the community.

The logic of Jesus suggests that the world is not about maintaining top-down power but about the emergence of a resilient bottom-up sort of power that creates solidarity and ties working people together. Jesus's way of life leads to stronger communities where productivity and creativity are valued rather than dominance, and where power-sharing and a sense of community shape our economic relationships. The goal is not integrating minorities into some dominant status quo but bringing together and organizing the majority of people facing devastating realities of growing economic inequality that go hand-in-hand with worshiping the wrong god. For Christians, the choice seems clear: gathered by the grace of Jesus or pulled apart by the power of Caesar.[34]

QUESTIONS FOR REFLECTION AND DISCUSSION

1. How are dominant economic assumptions shaping the Christian life and images of the divine?

2. What does Jesus have to do with Wall Street?

3. What difference might a deeper understanding of the struggle of Jesus vs. Caesar make to the lives of the 99 percent who have to work for a living?

Chapter 5

THE WAY, THE TRUTH, AND THE LIFE?

On Interreligious and Other Dialogues

Failure to understand and engage the tension between life-giving and malignant religion has not just kept life-giving Christianity from flourishing. It has also prevented life-giving interreligious relationships from taking off. Who would want to be in conversation with a malignant religion that seeks to dominate the world, except those who also use their religious traditions for domination? While other religious traditions are also implicated in histories of domination,[1] our concern with Jesus and Christianity in this book implies that we start with ourselves and rethink our cherished assumption that Christians have exclusive access to the "way, the truth, and the life" (John 14:6).

Depending on how Jesus's claim to be the way, the truth, and the life is understood, interreligious engagements may be off the table. If Jesus is right and everybody else is wrong, there is no need for dialogue or conversation. In this case, all that is needed is a firm proclamation and a push. This has been the attitude toward other religions time and again in the history of Christianity, and sometimes the proclamation and the push together turned deadly. In the case of the Spanish Conquest of the sixteenth century, for instance, even though the missionaries were in some

93

cases prevented from evangelizing indigenous peoples by force, resistance to missionary proclamation could be eliminated by the use of force.[2]

On the other hand, there are well-meaning but somewhat naive forms of interreligious dialogue, framed by the assumption that we are all alike. In this case, the difference between Jesus and Caesar would be a matter of dialogue and negotiation, with the expectation that there is more similarity than difference. This is, of course, more than a modern problem, as Christianity under the conditions of empire has often tried to accommodate to the powers that be. In recent times, some have even suggested that we start an interreligious dialogue between Christianity and neoliberal capitalism, since the latter has taken on the form of a religion. Yet if the premise of dialogue is that we are more alike than different and that we need to find ways to coexist peacefully, we may have a problem. The Jesus of the Gospels, as we have seen in previous chapters, is quite clear that our conversations definitely do not mean endless concessions and anything goes.

Peace is, of course, what most well-meaning people would prefer to conflict. But Caesar's idea of peace, the so-called *Pax Romana*, came with its own set of problems. The Roman peace was established on a particular kind of top-down relationship that ran from the winners of history to the losers. This Roman peace demanded the concord and the agreement of its subjects.[3] This did not necessarily imply that people had to give up their identities—Jews could remain Jewish and Greeks could remain Greeks (as Paul indicates in 1 Cor 9:19-22). But it meant that all had to respect and submit to Caesar and his power. Not all peace is therefore the same, and not all peace is equally desirable. The prophet Jeremiah notes the problem with top-down peace: "They have treated the wound of my people carelessly, saying, 'Peace, peace,' when there is no peace" (Jeremiah 6:14; 8:11).

As we rethink the relationship between Christianity and other religious traditions, another matter needs to be spelled out. Within the same religious traditions there are tensions that also matter. I am not talking primarily about differences between Christian denominations like Methodists and Roman Catholics; I am talking about differences arising between people within the same denomination. In Nazi Germany, for instance, there were Christians of the same denomination who supported Hitler and others who did not. The difference between these camps was decisive and in many ways mattered more than denominational differences. Likewise, there were people of other religious traditions who were divided along the same lines. This resulted in situations where people of different religions might have more in common than people of the same faith tradition—a Christian resisting Hitler, for instance, would likely have had more in common with a person of Jewish faith than with another Christian who supported the Nazi regime.

No matter how we interpret Jesus's claim to be the way, the truth, and the life, this claim is made about Jesus and not about Christianity; it is made about an embodied way of life rather than an isolated idea. In the Johannine traditions, where this claim is found, truth is performative rather than cognitive—linked to action rather than mere knowledge. This kind of truth is not only in people's mind but it is liberating for flesh and blood people (John 8:32).[4] Christianity cannot claim ownership of Jesus by default, since it does not control Jesus's way of life. And, if Jesus's liberative way of life is somehow related to the truth, we will not and cannot claim that everything is equally true: Caesar and the way of repressive power will still be wrong after all.

> No matter how we interpret Jesus's claim to be the way, the truth, and the life, this claim is made about Jesus and not about Christianity; it is made about an embodied way of life rather than an isolated idea.

THE CONFLICT OF INTERRELIGIOUS DIALOGUE: NOT WHAT WE THOUGHT

Dominant images of the truth are often unilateral. Most empires and many faith communities today are convinced that truth is a possession, they have it, and there is no alternative. For this reason, empires usually do not invite dialogue and conversation, and if they do, they supply all the answers. If Jesus's claim to be the truth is seen in this light, there is indeed no need for dialogue and conversation on anything, least of all religion. The infamous bumper sticker describes the situation: "God said it, I believe it, that settles it."

As we have seen so far, however, empires have a tendency to define the truth of Christianity in ways that have little to do with Jesus because they endorse various forms of top-down power that stand in contrast to the kind of power Jesus embodies and represents. As a result, for the past two thousand years, when empires were in charge, the winning logic of Caesar had christological effects: Jesus was made to look just like him. Not surprisingly, many who embrace the sensibility featured in the aforementioned bumper sticker frequently confuse God and Caesar.

Moreover, Caesar always had the means to enforce his truth and rarely hesitated to use them. These means included rhetoric and persuasion, a staff of philosophers and schools, religious influence, and if all that was not enough, coercion and violence. It is no coincidence that in the final clash between the truth of Caesar and the truth of Jesus, Jesus ends up on one of the many crosses designed to eliminate political dissidents, those who fundamentally disagreed with the empire. An old hymn that is not found in most contemporary hymnals captures the difference in this way: "Truth forever on a scaffold, wrong forever on a throne."[5] There remains a fundamental difference between the truth of Jesus and the truth of Caesar.

While Caesar might have assumed that the truth of Jesus would come to an end with his crucifixion, the opposite was the case. Jesus's followers took his truth from Jerusalem to the ends of the earth, continuing the clash of deeply held convictions and truths. That the Apostle Paul spent his life in and out of prison and was most likely killed by the empire was not based on a harmless misunderstanding: the Romans understood the potential dangers of the Christian message only too well. While the dominant truth-claims of Roman power sought to repress Jesus's alternative take on reality as much as possible, the truth embodied in Jesus and the

Jesus traditions kept the early Christians going—so much so that some people were willing to lay down their lives for it.

The clash between the truth of Caesar and the truth of Jesus is not merely a matter of content. It is also a matter of form, as Jesus did not enforce his truth like Caesar, and neither did the early Christians. It was only later, when Christianity had more fully adapted to the respective principalities and powers, that the truth of Christianity was enforced like the dominant truth. An ancient image of the late fifth century shows the Christ in imperial uniform, holding the Johannine text about the way, the truth, and the life, and a cross over his shoulders like a sword, stepping on lion and snake.[6] In due time, institutions like the Inquisition would defend truth by means of torture and even the execution of those considered heretics.

Jesus's famous claim to be the truth has a distinctly different flavor than Caesar's claim to be the kind of truth that settles things without need for conversation and engagement with other perspectives. In the Gospels, Jesus often initiates conversation, sometimes uncovering truth in unlikely places. We already discussed the story of the Syrophoenician woman, whose arguments make Jesus change his mind (Mark 7:24-30, see chapter 1). In his parables, too, Jesus finds truth in the actions of ordinary people, shepherds, fishermen, women baking bread, and working people struggling with debt: they are the ones who are speaking through Jesus and their truth contradicts the dominant take on reality proclaimed and enforced from the top down.

Examples include the logic of the shepherd who goes out to look for the one lost sheep, or the logic of the father who surprises the expectations of the time by welcoming home a son who disappointed him, despite his older son's understandable pushback (Luke 15:11-32), or even the despised foreigner who takes care of a victim better than members of the violated man's own people (the parable of the so-called "good Samaritan," Luke 10:25-37). To be sure, Christianity did not always fully understand the meaning of all of this, which is why it would be wrong to equate specific forms of Christianity with the truth.

In some cases, others understood Jesus's truth better than the disciples of Jesus themselves, like Samaritans such as the so-called "woman at the well" (John 4:1-42). Jesus notes that even the stones would shout out if the followers of Jesus failed to recognize and proclaim the truth (Luke 19:40). This kind of truth is related to what we might call *the truth of the multitude*, which is based on collective wisdom that in this case would include many of the ancient Jewish traditions on which Jesus relied.[7]

While the truth of the multitude is inclusive of the masses with which Jesus connected, it also has some exclusive traits—undermining the idea that anything goes. The truth of the multitude is not the same as populism, which is informed by the kind of popular opinion that is manipulated by demagogues. Could this be what is expressed in the second sentence that follows Jesus's claim to be the way, the truth, and the life: "No one comes to the Father except through me" (John 14:6)? No matter how open Jesus was to the truth he found at work among the people of his time, he draws the line where empire shapes the truth and people's minds. While speaking blessing to the poor, he pronounces condemnation to the rich: "Woe to you who are rich!" (Luke 6:24). Jesus and his followers were aware that the rich all too often get to where they are on the backs of the poor, manipulating them in the process.

Once again, truth is not found in places of privilege but in places of struggle and resilient suffering. The Lutheran tradition contains some notion of this when, in the Heidelberg Disputation, Jesus's claim that no one comes to the Father except through him is tied to the crucified Christ, in conscious opposition to the triumphant Christ.[8]

Jesus's response to the disciples' repeated quarrel about who is the greatest among them (see, e.g., Mark 9:33-37) reframes truth and moves it from the top to the bottom, thus broadening the horizons of what is real and spelling out what is not. As it turns out, Samaritans and tax collectors who support the least of these can become allies, and religious and political officials who do not support the least of these cannot. Here, possibilities for interreligious dialogue can take off in new directions that might turn out to be life-giving.

WRONG GOD: WHAT DIFFERENCE DOES IT MAKE?

It is often assumed that Christianity was one uniform religion at its beginning and that diversity of perspective developed only later. Part of the blame for Christian diversity and plurality is sometimes directed at the Protestant Reformers of the sixteenth century, who supposedly split a church that was more or less uniform until that time. In reality, of course, there were many other earlier splits, including the most significant separation of the churches in the East and the West in the eleventh century. More importantly, however, what is overlooked here is that there was no uniform formulation of Christian faith until the fourth century, when the Roman ruler Constantine called the Council of Nicaea (and even then, there were always locally divergent forms of belief and practice).

The New Testament church was at least as diverse as the books that made it into the canon. Even the four Gospels display differences and embody a kind of diversity with the Gospel of John providing the voice that is most different from the so-called Synoptic Gospels. There, Jesus gives long speeches that are not found in any of the other Gospels, including the claim to be the way, the truth, and the life. Many other first-century Christian writings that did not make it into the canon, like the first letter of Clement and the so-called Didache, remind us of even greater diversity that existed in the beginnings of Christianity. As Ernst Käsemann has famously pointed out, the New Testament canon does not establish the unity of the early church but rather its plurality.[9]

When Christianity became more settled and sanctioned in the empire, two things happened: while Christianity became more streamlined and unified, the old contrast between Jesus and Caesar grew weaker. This process, which came into its own with the Emperor Constantine's conversion to Christianity in the fourth century, changed the understanding of truth operative in Christianity as well. While up to that point diversity and truth seemed compatible to various degrees, after the official imperial embrace of Christian faith things changed. At the point when Constantine declared himself the sole emperor over the Roman Empire (having defeated his opponent and co-emperor Licinius), Christianity became an important player shoring up and reclaiming the uniformity of the empire.

As we saw earlier, Constantine's efforts to establish a more singular form of acceptable Christianity led to the domestication of Jesus according to the dominant images of God at the time. The Jesus whom the Nicene Creed declared to be of the same substance as God was removed from the life and the ministry of Jesus. It is no accident that the Nicene Creed does not reference the life and ministry of Jesus—and neither do other creeds like the Apostles' Creed, the Athanasian Creed, or the Chalcedonian Creed.

The truth of the empire is clean and unilateral, as well as easily definable in terms of top-down power, deployed in the hands of dominant persons and groups who are able to wield it unilaterally. By contrast, the truth of the life and ministry of Jesus is messy, replete with passion, confrontations, siding with the least of these, and ultimately death. Even in the Gospel of John and other Johannine writings, where truth is elevated more strongly than in the Synoptic Gospels, there is a sense of this messiness. Truth is something that happens on the way; truth is done (John 3:21; 1 John 1:6)—a notion of truth that is closer to popular Jewish thinking than to the ideals of Hellenistic elites.[10] Most importantly, this truth has to be embodied in a particular history—the history of the conflict between Jesus and Caesar.

In contrast to the truth of Jesus, unilateral top-down truth—the truth of the powerful—seems unable to register what goes on in the concrete messiness of reality. That the least of these are forgotten is not just an exceptional accident or an unfortunate oversight, but part of how the truth of the powerful functions. And when the least of these are taken into account, they are often only an afterthought (like the soup kitchen that opens after worship is done) or understood in terms of the dominant system, and thus rendered deficient. Where this unilateral truth rules supreme, support for the least of these amounts to gathering them up into the dominant system, just as the Nicene Creed did with Jesus.

> That the least of these are forgotten is not just an exceptional accident or an unfortunate oversight, but part of how the truth of the powerful functions.

In sum, truth that is unilaterally proclaimed from above either usurps or excludes the majority of humanity and their on-the-ground religious traditions and commitments—the forced inclusion and the forced exclusion of others are both part of the logic empire.[11] The picture looks even more skewed if we stop and ask in whose interest this truth functions: benefiting from top-down truth are surprisingly small groups of elites who assume that they are able to speak for all—like the Roman emperors and their client kings like Herod—those who are able to shape the rest of the world in their own image. This dynamic applies not only to those who are very different—like the peasants in Jesus's Galilee—but also to those closer to home like the majority of the citizens of Rome, who would experience constant pressure to conform, toe the line, and go along with the imperial flow.

The nationalism that often accompanies empire might serve as an example for what is going on, then and now: nationalism demands that everyone conform to the values of a nation, often determined by a few ideologues. In the United States, this can be seen in one version of what is commonly called "family values," a surprisingly narrow idea of what a family is, rooted in the value world of the white suburban 1950s experience rather than in the long and deep traditions of Christian faith. These so-called family values are all too often marked by nuclear-family patriarchy (think the assumed authority and superiority of golden-age, in-charge television fathers), limited agency of women, capitalist ideas of private ownership, and homophobia. Those who accommodate to such ideals receive certain benefits such as feelings of protection, safety, and belonging, but they also must submit to what is defined as common interest. This common interest, however, is not as common as it might seem, since it is mostly defined by the interests of the ruling classes. The common interest of the Third Reich's take on German nationalism, for instance, was closely tied to the interests of big industry and the power brokers who put themselves in control.[12]

Racism is fueled ·by similar and resonant dynamics, as it serves the interests of the powerful dominant class. Racist workers who vote for racist politicians, for instance, tend to assume that their interests are being served. What they overlook, however, is that their racism functions to distort their own lives, covering up, for instance, key differences between white workers and white employers. As a result, racist workers are often voting against their own interests without knowing it, as they are likely to share more in common with black workers than with their white employers. This includes all the pressures that make work-life challenging today, like the limitation of benefits, ever-increasing pressure to perform, lack of shared governance, and so on. Which side would you guess embodies the truth of Jesus (vs. the truth of Caesar)?

It is not hard to see that interreligious dialogue cannot flourish in this climate, and so interreligious dialogue often gets stuck in the controlled exchange of ideas that are sanctioned by the word-policing status quo. What gets lost here is more than just interreligious dialogue. What is lost is the heart of the Jewish and the Christian traditions themselves, which cannot be pressed into the system of dominant empire religions. Worshiping the wrong god—the god of dominant power and nationalism—forecloses on those conversations with religious others where a shared recognition of pain, struggle, and the power of resilience might lead to a better life for all.

WRONG GOD, RIGHT GOD: THE STRUGGLE CONTINUES

The Gospel of John, in which Jesus claims to be the way, the truth, and the life, has often been characterized as dualistic, that is, dividing the world into polar opposites. And John does feature various dualisms, between light and darkness, love and hate, good and evil, truth and lies. At first sight, this attitude does not sit well with efforts to establish interreligious or other dialogues. Would making distinctions between true and false gods not create more barriers between religions? Would it not be better to keep an open mind rather than to draw lines in the sand?

Dialogue, however, is not only openness but also an acknowledgment of limits. Torturers and their victims, to use an extreme example, cannot enter into a dialogue. More specifically, the victims of torture must refuse dialogue in order to defeat the goals of the torturer. The same is true when other incompatible positions clash, particularly when one side benefits from a marked power differential. During the rule of Nazi fascism in Germany, for instance, anti-fascist Christians could not enter into a dialogue with fascist Christians without a clear understanding of the boundaries and limits. The same is true today for those who suggest conversations between capitalism (as a quasi-religion) and traditional forms of faith. An old German saying notes that in situations of great danger and need, the middle road leads to death.[13] "Reaching across the aisle" can be self-defeating when the power differentials are too great and lives are at stake, and merely "adding cross to crown" seems hardly enough.[14]

> Dialogue is not only openness but also an acknowledgment of limits.

When considering limits in terms of interreligious dialogue, we should understand that the limits are not always where we expect them to be. The lines that need to be drawn are not necessarily between different religions but within religious traditions themselves. As we pointed out in chapter 1, the question of true and false gods is not necessarily a conflict between religions but points to the tensions within particular religious traditions. In other words, the fundamental question for Christians is not whether Christians and the adherents of other religions believe in the same God but whether Christians and other Christians believe in the same God.

The conflict in the Gospel of John appears to be a conflict within a religious tradition itself: rather than presenting a challenge to others who are completely different, the challenge is presented to those who belong to one's own faith lineage but who hold power and who have made common cause with a particular dominant status quo. Very unfortunately and misleadingly, the Gospel of John calls the dominant opponents of Jesus "the Jews." However, this term does not designate all Jews but certain leaders of the community who are in positions of power. At stake is not a conflict between Christianity and Judaism but between competing forms of the faith of Israel and adherents to traditions that are closely related.[15]

The dualism of Jesus in the Gospel of John is instructive for how we might rethink dialogue. The tension between truth and lies, for instance, is not between absolute claims of truth but between embodied ways of life. In John, truth is always embodied—it is either done, or not done (John 3:21; 1 John 1:6)—and it liberates (John 8:32). We might put this insight together with a famous passage in another part of Johannine literature, 1 John 4:1-2: "Beloved, do not believe every spirit, but test the spirits to see whether they are from God; for many false prophets have gone out into the world. By this you know the Spirit of God: every spirit that confesses that Jesus Christ has come in the flesh is from God." The criterion for testing the spirits and for figuring out the difference between truth and lies is not an idea of Jesus but the embodied Jesus, the one who has a particular history, who lives in a particular way, builds specific relationships, and so on.

The line within one's own religion is, therefore, not drawn narrowly. In contrast to Caesar's unilateral approach to truth, early Christianity seems to have embodied truth as having plural forms and open-ended shapes, while also drawing some lines of distinction. In the book of Acts, Christians are considered to be the people of "the way," which is the way of Jesus Christ embodied in history. Christian uniformity is not necessary—there are Jewish Christians in Jerusalem and Gentile Christians elsewhere, and there are disagreements within each of these groups as well. What holds them together is not a narrow set of ideas but the difference between Jesus and Caesar, expressed in the Lord's Prayer for God's kingdom to come and God's will to be done—as opposed to Caesar's kingdom and will.

After having done some housecleaning within the Christian traditions, what about interreligious relationships? Where is the struggle taking place there?

The Christian history of mission can help us see what is at stake in particular interreligious interactions, starting with how *not* to engage others. Many past examples of mission show the problems with embracing the unilateral truth of empire. Converting people aided by fire and the sword is part of the problem. Keep in mind whose mission this might be, as there are no records that Jesus ever converted anyone by fire and sword, and Jesus never encouraged anyone else to do so. In fact, when one of Jesus's supporters pulls his sword in the final confrontation with empire, Jesus tells him to but it back (Matt 12:52; only the Gospel of John identifies the person with Peter [John 18:10]). Clearly, the Christian history of mission demands that we establish some limits and draw some lines, as empire's influence on religion through the centuries has been mostly toxic to productive interreligious relationships.

Yet even the softer missions of more recent centuries tend to perpetuate the problem. Both the sixteenth-century Spanish theologian Bartolomé de Las Casas and the nineteenth-century German theologian Friedrich Schleiermacher assumed that mission by force was wrong and that the way of Jesus was a "gentle and gracious way," proceeding by attraction rather than coercion.[16]

Schleiermacher's example is particularly important because he was also one of the theologians who helped Christianity accept and appreciate other religions. He acknowledged that all religions had some level of God-consciousness and he found value in other religions, opening up the possibility for interreligious dialogue. Yet Schleiermacher also operated with a clear taxonomy of religion, according to which some religions were of a higher order than others, with his own brand of Protestant Christianity, no surprise, being at the top. As father of liberal theology, Schleiermacher's vision was that Christianity would spread through attraction, letting its natural superiority do its work. His thoughts were based on the conviction that what he considered the "higher" would always attract the "lower."[17] In this way, Schleiermacher's liberal God continued the spirit of the empire.

The mission to Native Americans in the United States illustrates perhaps most tellingly where the lines need to be drawn when it comes to interreligious encounters, and what is at stake in the struggle between Jesus and Caesar, between the right and the wrong god. The surprising twist of this history is that many missionaries who promoted dominant interests and ended up on the side of the wrong god did not personally benefit much from their own work. George Tinker tells the story of the missionaries to the Native Americans, who got neither rich nor powerful through their missionary efforts but whose work—mostly without being aware of it—created the conditions for others to get rich and powerful. The key problem, it seems, was that the missionaries' captivity to dominant images of truth did not allow them to learn from the truth of the native peoples, to take them seriously, and to form mutual relationships.[18]

As a result, even some of the most laudable efforts, like providing education, backfired. The mission schools for Native Americans, for instance, that might be considered offering positive support for families and their children, turned out to be places of reeducation in the dominant faith's truths, facilitated by removing children from their families. Likewise, schools established in Latin America in the nineteenth century by Protestant missionaries were more often instrumental in preparing people for the tasks of economic development than for the traditions of Jesus—a situation that was only gradually reversed in the wake of the liberation movements of the twentieth century.[19]

Néstor Míguez talks about *inclusive-exclusivism* in his reflections on what he calls the Christian revolution. The question is not whether we should be inclusive, exclusive, or both. The question is what are the options of a movement of oppressed people struggling for liberation. What Míguez says about Paul helps us understand and broaden a dynamic that can be observed in the Jesus movement as well: what appears to be exclusive about the early Christian movements is that they had to be clear about where they stood over against the dominant powers, but in terms of this standpoint, these movements were inclusive of everyone. This produces new forms of social relations that offer an alternative to "'the subordinating inclusion' of the imperial ideology."[20] The interesting question for us is where this line of exclusion is being drawn and where inclusion needs to be the order of the day.

Traditional forms of interreligious dialogue used to draw the line in terms of particular religions, like Christianity vs. Islam, or Buddhism vs. Judaism. Yet these religions are quite complex and there are lines of division that run within each of them. The dividing line between Jesus and Caesar reminds us of one such conflict within Christianity itself, as Christianity was increasingly reframed as the religion of Caesar. The liberal effort to avoid drawing hard lines does not resolve the problem but makes it worse because it leads to an implicit endorsement of whatever religious tradition is dominant. Declaring all religions as basically the same overlooks the decisive differences that continue to be very real, both for good and for ill (and usually defining others on our own terms). The problem is that this approach, despite the fact that it seeks to be open and even welcoming to others, feeds back into dominant understandings of truth.

RIGHT GOD: "RESCUE US FROM THE EVIL ONE"

The final petition of the Lord's Prayer (Matt 6:13) reads: "And do not bring us to the time of trial but rescue us from the evil one." It is not hard to see that this petition is not spoken from a position of dominance. Those who have to be worried about trials are either the ones who have gotten in trouble with the law, or they are the underdogs, those who worry about unjust trials even though they may have done nothing wrong.

This is how African Americans in the United States experience the structures of empire. It is well known that African Americans and other minorities are stopped in traffic more frequently than those who are white, due to the common practice of racial profiling. Sometimes these stops escalate. But that's just the tip of the iceberg. More racial minorities find themselves in prison because they are often treated more harshly by courts, judges, and juries. Even death row is disproportionately populated by minorities.[21]

The structures of empire are also at work in the harassment of those who practice non-Christian religions in the United States, particularly by

Muslim women who wear the hijab (head scarf) or display other markers of their religious identity. No interreligious dialogue makes sense, therefore, without a closer look at how power flows, and how this power is shaped by dominant religious sensitivities and suppressions.

In these contexts of prejudice, harassment, and mistreatment a God who sets a different example can make a tremendous difference. Not doling out harsher judgment to some people more than others and not falsely accusing them is a start, but the demands of justice go deeper. In the ancient Jewish traditions from which Jesus draws, justice is not merely maintaining neutrality but taking the side of those who have been harmed and integrating them back into the community.[22] In chapter 1, we noted the distinction between the Roman goddess Justitia's supposed neutrality (an ideal that helped Caesar more than anyone else) and Jesus's commitment to justice for the rest of the population.

This Jewish notion of justice that emerges from some of the Hebrew traditions, picked up by Jesus and early Christianity, makes for different interreligious encounters, specifically in regard to those religions that are less prominent or have been repressed. Neutrality and fairness are preferable to prejudice and bias, but that is not enough. Genuine encounters with less prominent and repressed religious traditions are not optional; such encounters are required for adherents of dominant religious traditions in order to understand who they are, what they believe, and where they might need some work.

While many Christians in the United States suspect Muslims of being violent (fed by media images of terrorism and violent forms of Islamic faith), for instance, encounters with actual Muslims challenge those suspicions. In addition, such encounters can jog the memory of a thousand-year-old history of Christian violence against Muslims, all the way back to the Crusades of the Middle Ages, that continues today in various forms. For Christians, this means not only that contemporary uses of the term *crusade* are no longer acceptable but that the kinds of relationships that go along with modern ideas of crusading also have to change. Rethinking Christian-Muslim relationships based on recalling repressive relationships would make a tremendous difference, not only in the United States but also around the globe.

What about the second half of Jesus's petition, the rescue from evil or from the evil one (the Greek text can be read in both ways)? The Gospel of Matthew (the version of the Lord's Prayer in the Gospel of Luke does not contain this part) directs us to the reality of evil that would have been experienced by Jesus's contemporaries. These experiences include everyday matters like suffering, illness, evil people, and evil desires, which are mentioned in Jewish texts written at the time of Jesus.[23]

While the experience of evil continues today, under the conditions of the Roman Empire the roots of this evil may have been more obvious to people. Peasants then could see that their suffering was caused by relationships of exploitation, and they were aware that those who perpetuated evil were the representatives of Roman power and the structures of empire and not merely evil individual actors. Today, so-called "structural evil" is usually more difficult to see, as political and economic relationships are less personal (there is no emperor or king and no chest of gold coins), and many people are simply not fully aware of their predicaments as long as they can max out their credit cards and leverage other forms of debt.

Lack of awareness of the root causes of structural evil leads to blaming the wrong people. Some Americans blame immigrants, for instance, when good employment opportunities are few and far between, rather than blaming companies who cut jobs and send them overseas. Likewise, certain religions are blamed for evil, like Islam for violence, Hinduism for social hierarchies like the caste system, Judaism (through historically anti-Semitic stereotypes) for financial woes, and most non-Christian religions for lack of respect for women.

A clearer sense of the roots of evil and the evil one, which a deeper interpretation of the life and ministry of Jesus can help us see, may ease the weight of misguided blame and suspicion plaguing interreligious relationships. Violence, social hierarchies, financial woes, and lack of respect for women are not the trademarks of other religions but deeply embedded in the unjust structures that our globalized societies have created— often with the help of distorted forms of religion, above all a distorted

Christianity that has been shaped by the power of Caesar more than by the power of Jesus.

A more thoughtful understanding of the roots of evil can also help people stop blaming themselves, a common condition under the conditions of empire, then as now. Peasants at Jesus's time were hardly poor because they were lazy or cursed, and the same is true for workers today who are forced to work minimum wage jobs (often more than one). And violence is rooted in deep political and economic structures that play off people against each other, often using religion as a pretext or a cover up. The so-called "clash of the civilizations" is based on these clashes at deeper levels. Investigations of how religions or civilizations clash without taking into account how these clashes are tied to political and economic power differentials are not only deficient but profoundly misleading.[24]

While religious traditions, Christianity included, can be (and have been) used for the purposes of evil, they also can be used for good. Maybe this is the point of praying for rescue from the evil one. The clash between Jesus and Caesar that continues today is not mirrored in a clash between different religions: especially in the United States, the location of this clash is within the various religions themselves, beginning with Christianity. This clash between Jesus and Caesar is best engaged when religions work together for the good against evil and when they join together in the search for the way, the truth, and the life, against lies and death. In recent times, this could be seen in the struggles against exploitation that led people of various faiths to pool their resources in the Occupy Wall Street movement or in forms of resistance like protests against the Dakota Access Pipeline project or in the Black Lives Matter movement.[25]

Working together against evil, people of various religions can learn about deeper images of power at work within their own traditions, without needing to claim that all religions are the same or that theirs is a superior form of faith. What ties them together is not primarily the identity of their religions but rather what Ephesians 6:12 presents as our common struggle, which is "not against enemies of blood and flesh, but against the rulers, against the authorities, against the cosmic powers of this present darkness, against the spiritual forces of evil in the heavenly places." That is where we find true images of God and rule out false images of God, and this is where the various religions can learn from each other.

Working together against evil, people of various religions can learn about deeper images of power at work within their own traditions, without needing to claim that all religions are the same or that theirs is a superior form of faith.

CONCLUSION: BEYOND DIALOGUE

What matters for Christians in considering Jesus as the way, the truth, and the life is how they are on the way together. In his commentary on that passage in the Gospel of John, Rudolf Bultmann notes that the journey is the destination and that the destination is reached in walking.[26] The truth of Jesus is tied to movement, embodiment, and life. As previous chapters have argued, this truth has political, material, and economic consequences. As people of faith travel along that way, the difference between Jesus and Caesar becomes clearer and clearer.

This line between Jesus and Caesar, as we saw earlier, runs within Christianity itself. Not anything goes, and Christians who worship top-down power and money are betraying Jesus, as no one can serve two masters. At the same time, people of other faiths who refuse to worship top-down power and money, who stand in solidarity with the exploited and the oppressed, will find themselves closer to Christians who follow the way of Jesus than to people of their own faiths who follow the way of Caesar. This affinity doesn't turn them into Christians, of course, but they can be fellow travelers who are able to appreciate the wisdom and the power of Jesus and a faith that makes a positive difference in the world.

Perhaps at this point in our shared history we need rethink the way we usually speak about inclusion and exclusion. While these terms are often thought of as mutually exclusive, they are brought together in Jesus's way

111

of life. On the one hand, Jesus actively broadens the circle of people to whom the good news is brought: the sick, the oppressed, the poor, and in some cases the circle is broadened for him when non-Jewish people connect with him (recall the Syrophoenician woman, the woman at the well, and a Roman centurion in Matthew 8:5-13). This is an important two-way street, since religious traditions have tendencies to become self-serving and narcissistic.

On the other hand, Jesus draws a line when it comes to those who use religion or faith for self-serving purposes and to oppress others (Matt 23:1-36). Once again, the line is not drawn between different religions but within religious traditions themselves. In other words, this line does not preclude interreligious encounters and dialogue. There are always limits to inclusion. Jesus does not seek to include or gather people into an unjust status quo: unlike Reinhold Niebuhr's Christian realism, he does not tell people to "accept the things they cannot change,"[27] but rather he prays for delivery from evil.

The difference between Jesus and Caesar is that the horizon is only truly broadened when, in addition to broadening moves, we also have the nerve to take a stand and draw a line. In order to do this, we need to develop some understanding of what we are up against: What are the sources of terror and destruction in our world? What is the evil from which we need to be delivered? What is the good? People of faith learn the answer not by speculation but by being on the way, embracing the truth that leads to liberation. This was, after all, the experience of Jesus's disciples as well, though it took years to understand, with perpetual failure and mistakes marking their path.

> The common struggle against evil leads us beyond what is commonly considered dialogue. Something more is required, and that is being on the road together, joining in the struggle together against whatever threatens life.

In sum, the common struggle against evil leads us beyond what is commonly considered dialogue. If we are up against Caesar and his empire—matters of life and death—we cannot continue with business as usual. Engaging in dialogue and trying to understand others and their religious traditions is not enough when Rome is burning. Something more is required, and that is being on the road together, joining in the struggle together against whatever threatens life, and thus developing a better sense for what is life-giving in situations that are death-dealing.

None of this can be figured out in the heads of theologians or in the comfort of our sanctuaries. In the Jewish and Christian traditions, from Abraham and Moses to Jesus and Paul, theology was for the most part done on the road, in movement and action.[28] And as Jesus told his disciples: "Follow me"—into the world.

QUESTIONS FOR REFLECTION AND DISCUSSION

1. How has the quest for religious truth been death-dealing? How has it been life-giving?

2. Have you experienced respectful encounters with other religious traditions? If not, what might be the reasons?

3. What are ways in which your community might engage more deeply in productive interreligious encounters?

CONCLUSION

KEEP FIGHTING

Why keep fighting Caesar? Why can't we just get along? Isn't it time to put the conflict to rest and move on? Terms like *forgiveness* and *reconciliation*[1] have currency today, and in politics there is always talk about "reaching across the aisle."

Idealized images of Jesus that are in many people's minds seem to concur. One of these idealized images of Jesus is all about love: "Jesus loves you," says the bumper sticker (and most Christians concur). If shallow notions of love suggest that Jesus accepts people "just as they are," why wouldn't Jesus also accept Caesar just as he is? Another idealized image of Jesus pushes shallow images of forgiveness and reconciliation. This Jesus is all about "forgive and forget." Why would Jesus not just forgive the Romans for torturing and executing him on the cross and forget the trauma?[2]

The Jesus whom we have encountered in this book hardly matches these idealized images. The love and forgiveness he embodies are not shallow, they have an edge and are powerful enough to unmake empires over time. Jesus's love can be tough and pose challenges; even when loving someone he can push back. Caesar is not home free to rule with impunity. Jesus's forgiveness is inextricably tied up with liberation and the taking of sides, as no one can serve two masters. And there can be no negotiating or reconciliation with evil.

115

Of course, someone might suggest that in the end, we are all Caesar. Aren't we all both, a little bit oppressor and oppressed? Wasn't Martin Luther right when he insisted that Christians are all justified and sinners at the same time (*simul iustus et peccator*)? While there is some truth to this, this neglects something central to Jesus's life, teaching, and ministry: the larger structures of oppression and sin. Caesar is not just some powerful individual but represents the Roman Empire and all empires where power is located at the top and inequality is the order of the day.

While there is much concern about structural evil and oppression today, in the Roman Empire the structures were often more visible. To be sure, certain pressures are visible today as well, for instance in unjustified police shootings of young black people and increasing number of shootings in schools and other public places, but the underlying structures go mostly unrecognized and are therefore rarely addressed.[3]

In the Roman Empire, political conquest and economic exploitation belonged together and were evident, for instance, in the occupying forces. "The Roman legionary soldier was at the same time an economic pioneer," according to Klaus Wengst, carrying both his weapons for fighting and tools for building.[4] In the United States, on the other hand, our own soldiers in full combat gear are less visible to the general population because they mostly operate overseas, and there is no occupying force on US soil. Even the increasing militarization of the police force in the United States is hardly encountered by the majority of the population, as it is mostly brought to bear in minority settings or against protests.

Our sense of exploitation is also fairly limited, as it is not always clear whether it even exists (the poor and the unemployed are blamed instead) or where it might be rooted. Unlike the tax collectors and client kings of old, corporate America is generally seen as benevolent or at least innocent; politicians may attract more blame but they are rarely linked to notions of economic exploitation. Yet less visibility does not mean that things are less real, just the opposite.

REVELATION

When people of faith talk about revelation, they often think of spectacular visions or experiences that communicate things totally new and never before encountered. Yet revelation in the life and ministry of Jesus might be better understood in terms of disclosing the difference that God makes here and now.[5] This includes a fresh sense of what we are up against as well as what we are fighting for. The struggle between Jesus and Caesar is about revelation in this particular sense, and there can be no revelation without understanding what is at stake in this struggle.

Jesus, praying for God's kingdom to come, exposes the empire of Caesar for what it is. Those who continue to pray with him for God's kingdom might develop an understanding that this kingdom turns on its head any and all kingdoms and empires in all the ways that we described in this book: top-down power turns into bottom up, competition turns into solidarity, self-centeredness turns into community, and neutrality turns into taking sides with the oppressed.

When Jesus refuses the temptation of embracing top-down power, revelation happens. When people realize the fundamental difference between the power of Satan and the power of God, revelation happens. This difference may not be totally new and unheard of, but developing a deeper sense of the struggle and of the need to take sides makes all the difference in the world. In light of this revelation, the time-honored notion of "making a personal decision for Jesus Christ" is turned back from its head to its feet and gains a whole new meaning and urgency.

The implications are wide-ranging, challenging even our deepest and most cherished images of God, including the ones that for centuries have been accepted as most logical and most rational. Perhaps the most widely accepted definition of God is the one developed by Anselm of Canterbury in the eleventh century who famously defined God as "something than which nothing greater can be thought."[6] If God is perceived in terms of those in power, in the image of Caesar rather than in the image of Jesus, this definition fails us. Even though Anselm's God is no tyrant because that God is bound by the law of justice,[7] it looks like Anselm hands the victory to Caesar rather than Jesus.

When we look for God, do we really need to keep staring up into the sky, toward the corner offices in the high rises, or toward the tallest steeples? What if we started to look down and around us instead, taking note

117

of the struggles and sufferings of life, where Jesus spent his life? Might we consider different definitions of God, for instance as "that than which nothing smaller (or more resilient) can be perceived"?

Here, what theologians call "general revelation" and "special revelation" clash. General revelation, that which supposedly can be deduced from status quo reason and its views of what is natural, tends to say one thing: God must be at the top, in control. Special revelation, on the other hand, that which is found in many of the biblical writings and in the Gospels, seems to say something else: God is at work from the bottom up. No easy reconciliation between the two positions is possible, and we may need to learn to live with this tension to find our place.

The conflict of Jesus vs. Caesar and the related revelation is perhaps best expressed in the Lord's Prayer. This prayer is straightforward and simple, as we have seen: food for hungry people, forgiveness of debt, resistance against evil, and the justice of God's rule. Of course, the empire promises all that as well, but we need to take a very close look at whether it delivers or not.

For almost forty years, neoliberal capitalism has promised us that a rising tide will lift all boats and that if the wealthy are doing better, everyone is doing better, too. During those decades, the wealthy have indeed done better than ever before in history, as eight individuals now have as much wealth as half of the world's population,[8] but what about the rest of humanity and the planet? As we have seen, more than a third of children in the United States are living near the poverty line, and many of them are going to bed hungry, and climate change is upon us, affecting those with fewer resources first.

Overall, poverty has been on the rise rather than on the decline even in the United States, and while the jobless rate is relatively low, the quality of jobs and pay and benefits are constantly deteriorating. Indebtedness has grown to new heights, and the way justice is practiced in the present has led to the largest number of people incarcerated in the United States in the history of the world, while white-collar crime is often acquitted with a slap on the wrist. All this resembles the time-honored ways of Caesar and the promises of the Roman Empire. The way of Jesus Christ is different, and his promises are not pies in the sky.

POWER AND SOLIDARITY

The tension between Jesus and Caesar would be misunderstood if it were conceived as a tension between power and the divestment from power. Jesus does not preach divestment from power; rather, he embodies a fundamentally different form of power. Jesus's power is tied up with the solidarity of people, starting with local communities. Jesus's power is relational, but it stands in stark contrast to the relational power of Caesar: in Rome, the relational power of the patronage system brought together the elites and tied them to the emperor. In Jesus's life, relational power brings together the people and ties them to the "least of these."

> Jesus's power is relational, but it stands in stark contrast to the relational power of Caesar: in Rome, the relational power of the patronage system brought together the elites and tied them to the emperor. In Jesus's life, relational power brings together the people and ties them to the "least of these."

Here, solidarity turns into what we are calling deep solidarity. It starts with those who experience the greatest pressures of our times in their own bodies: racial, ethnic, and sexual minorities; women; undocumented immigrants; and the massive number of children living below the poverty line. Deep solidarity continues as a force by reminding the rest of the population who ultimately benefits from the empires of this world: a fairly small minority who seeks to control not only politics and economics but also religion, culture, ways of life, and even our deepest feelings and relationships.

Deep solidarity does not require that all who are in solidarity are alike. It is just the opposite: as deep solidarity helps us understand that most of us are part of the 99 percent rather than the 1 percent, it depends on people using their differences to make a difference. Even the limited power of those who are better off can be put to productive use—men who realize that what is happening to women affects us all can use their male privilege to fight patriarchy, white people who realize that what is happening to racial minorities affects us all can use their white privilege to fight racism, middle-class people who have to work for a living and who realize that what is happening to workers affects us all can use their limited class privilege to fight exploitation, and so on. In the process, the various forms of privilege can and will be transformed into the different kind of power that Jesus embodies and represents. This is not just a theory—experiences of people involved in struggles for liberation confirm these dynamics.[9]

Deep solidarity has an objective and a subjective side: objectively, there is a sense that the 99 percent are in the same boat as they are benefiting less and less from the current economic system, due to rising inequality. Subjectively, we still need to pull together, and here we can learn from Jesus's ways of *organizing*—another and perhaps more appropriate name for what we traditionally call *discipleship*.

One more time we need to ask the question about the 1 percent. In the ancient collection of sayings of Jesus that scholars have called Q, one theme is the self-exclusion of the elites.[10] This is a problem that has been with us through the centuries: those at the top who have accumulated extreme wealth and power generally find it hard to embrace a logic that differs from the logic of Caesar. The good news is, however, that even the 1 percent can embrace the logic of Jesus and join the multitude of the 99 percent. This has happened consistently throughout history, though not frequently. One moving example is those among the 1 percent who, in response to the Occupy Wall Street movement's attention to the struggles of the 99 percent, publicly put themselves on the side of the 99 percent.[11]

Jesus in the Gospel of Matthew indicates the direction: "But strive first for the kingdom of God and his righteousness, and all these things will be given to you as well (Matt 6:33). The reference to "all these things" in this passage refers to the people's basic needs like clothing and food, and the way to secure them is not by providing charity but by working for God's kingdom and for justice, which is how the term *righteousness* should be translated in the conflict of Jesus vs. Caesar.

The good news is this: although empires continue to draw together massive concentrations of power, the power of Jesus could never be defeated and co-opted altogether. What we encounter here is bigger than us, not merely a set of ethical instructions or a recipe for a certain way of life. What we encounter here is the reality of God at work in Jesus, which can be fought and sometimes even suppressed, but which will always be with us, "to the end of this present age" (Matt 28:20).

QUESTIONS FOR REFLECTION AND DISCUSSION

1. Why can't we all just get along?

2. What are people of faith fighting against? What are people of faith fighting for?

3. What changes might be required in the lives of churches and communities of faith if we were to take seriously the tensions between Jesus and Caesar?

NOTES

PREFACE

1. In academic circles, dualisms and binaries are hotly contested. See Joerg Rieger, *Globalization and Theology* (Nashville: Abingdon Press, 2010), chapter 3. For another approach that employs the subversive nature of duality see Santiago Slabodsky, *Decolonial Judaism: Triumphal Failures of Barbaric Thinking*, New Approaches to Religion and Power (New York: Palgrave Macmillan, 2014). See also Brigitte Kahl, *Galatians Re-Imagined: Reading with the Eyes of the Vanquished* (Minneapolis: Fortress Press, 2010), 21–22, who notes that in Paul's theology a new polarity emerges between the old cosmos (Caesar) and the new creation that emerges in Christ, against an "evil order" and not "an evil Other."

INTRODUCTION

1. See, for instance, Amy-Jill Levine, *The Misunderstood Jew: The Church and the Scandal of the Misunderstood Jesus* (San Francisco: HarperSanFrancisco, 2006).

2. The term *religion*, as used in this book, refers not only to ideas but also to practices, both public and private, which are embodied in particular ways of life.

3. Native American theologians Clara Sue Kidwell, Homer Noley, and George E. Tinker, *A Native American Theology* (Maryknoll: Orbis Books, 2001), 62–84, note how the problem is not only Caesar—our images of Jesus have been thoroughly co-opted as well.

4. See also the detailed theological account of my book *Christ and Empire: From Paul to Postcolonial Times* (Minneapolis: Fortress Press, 2007). Empires, as I define the term in that book, are "massive concentrations of power that permeate all aspects of life and that cannot be controlled by any one actor alone" (2). While empires take on various forms in history, some more based on hard power, others on soft power, they share in common efforts to dominate life as a whole, not only economics and politics but also religion, culture, and personal life. As the power of empires is typically shared among elites, even in the Roman Empire, Caesar is, thus, not merely a powerful individual but the representative of more complex structures of power.

5. See the two-thousand-year history of empires shaping Christian images of Christ in Rieger, *Christ and Empire*.

6. According to a 2015 study of the Pew Research Center, young people in particular are moving away from religious affiliations. While 78 percent of the baby boomer generation report to be Christians, in older and younger millennials (born after 1981 and 1990) the numbers shrink to 57 and 56 percent. Numbers are not only dropping among mainline Christianity but among Evangelicals and Roman Catholics as well. See "America's Changing Religious Landscape," May 12, 2015, http://www .pewforum.org/2015/05/12/americas-changing-religious-landscape/.

7. The limits of the Jesus movement have been pointed out by various postcolonial critics, including R. S. Sugirtharajah, *Postcolonial Criticism and Biblical Interpretation* (Oxford: Oxford University Press, 2002), 88, who argues that "Jesus's alternative vision did not challenge or seek to radically alter the colonial apparatus." Precisely because some ambiguities remain, this statement seems to be claiming too much. For the resilience of silence see Tat-siong Benny Liew, "Haunting Silence: Trauma, Failed Orality, and Mark's Messianic Secret," *Psychoanalytic Mediations Between Marxist and Postcolonial Readings of the Bible*, ed. Tat-siong Benny Liew and Erin Runions (Atlanta: SBL Press, 2016), 99–127.

8. Note that this is also one of the major insights of postcolonial theory. The notion of ambivalence as challenge to empire is explored in my book *Christ and Empire*. In the words of Fernando Segovia, "Biblical Criticism and Postcolonial Studies: Toward a Postcolonial Optic," *The Postcolonial Bible*, ed. R. S. Sugirtharajah (Sheffield: Sheffield Academic Press, 1998), 61, "The structural binomial reality of imperialism and colonialism is never imposed or accepted in an atmosphere of absolute and undisturbed passivity."

9. For the numerous efforts to silence Latin American Liberation theology, see Philip Berryman, *Liberation Theology: Essential Facts about the Revolutionary Movement in Latin America and Beyond* (New York: Pantheon Books, 1987). According to a 1980 statement by the Committee of Santa Fe, linked to the policies of President Ronald Reagan, "U.S. policy must begin to counter (not react against) liberation theology" (3).

10. For a theological engagement with Jewish traditions in order to develop a deeper understanding of Jesus, see Jürgen Moltmann, *The Way of Jesus Christ: Christology in Messianic Dimensions*, trans. Margaret Kohl (Minneapolis: Fortress Press, 1993).

11. The Council of Chalcedon declared humanity and divinity in Christ to be without confusion and alteration and without division and separation.

12. Richard Horsley, *Jesus and Empire: The Kingdom of God and the New World Disorder* (Minneapolis: Fortress Press, 2003), 13, begins by comparing understanding the historical Jesus to the historical Martin Luther King Jr. Just as the latter could not have been understood without knowledge of the civil rights struggle, Jesus cannot be understood without knowing the struggles of his time.

13. A great deal of work has been done from the perspective of the margins, which has greatly expanded our view of Jesus and Paul. Examples include Miguel A. De La Torre, *The Politics of Jesús: A Hispanic Political Theology*, Religion in the Modern World (Lanham: Rowman and Littlefield, 2015); Richard Horsley, *Jesus and the Powers: Conflict, Covenant, and the Hope of the Poor* (Minneapolis: Fortress Press, 2011); Néstor O. Míguez, *The Practice of Hope: Ideology and Intention in 1 Thessalonians*,

trans. Aquíles Martínez (Minneapolis: Fortress Press, 2012); various African American and African, Latin American and Latino, and queer scholars, men and women, and many earlier scholars who investigated Jesus from the perspective of the working class, whose names are now forgotten (who knows the names of Cyrenus Osborne Ward or George Herron?) discussed in the inspiring work of David Burns, *The Life and Death of the Historical Jesus* (Oxford: Oxford University Press, 2013).

14. Reading the Bible in the context of movements, particularly with minority working people in union halls, has taught me a great deal over the years. See Joerg Rieger and Kwok Pui-lan, *Occupy Religion: Theology of the Multitude*, Religion in the Modern World (Lanham: Rowman and Littlefield, 2012); and Joerg Rieger and Rosemarie Henkel-Rieger, *Unified We Are a Force: How Faith and Labor Can Overcome America's Inequalities* (St. Louis: Chalice Press, 2012).

1. CHRISTIANS AS ATHEISTS?

1. According to *The New York Times*, Graham stated that the label *progressive* claimed by preachers like Barber is just another word for atheism. Laurie Goodstein, "Religious Liberals Sat Out of Politics for 40 Years Now They Want in the Game," *The New York Times*, June 10, 2017, https://www.nytimes.com/2017/06/10/us/politics/politics-religion-liberal-william-barber.html?_r=0.

2. Here is an interesting parallel to the Jewish philosopher Emmanuel Levinas, who interpreted Jewish Monotheism as atheism: "Monotheism marks a break with a certain conception of the Sacred. It neither unifies nor hierarchizes the numerous and numinous gods; instead it denies them. As regards the Divine which they incarnate, it is merely atheism." Emmanuel Levinas, *Difficult Freedom: Essays on Judaism*, trans. Seán Hand (Baltimore: Johns Hopkins University Press, 1990), 14–15.

3. In the same article of *The New York Times* by Laurie Goodstein, the Reverend Rich Nathan, pastor of a seventy-five-hundred–member church in Ohio, the largest church of the evangelical Vineyard denomination,

is quoted saying that few younger evangelicals are happy with the "old evangelical guard." https://www.nytimes.com/2017/06/10/us/politics /politics-religion-liberal-william-barber.html?_r=0.

4. Ancient Greek philosophy is foundational, and while there are nuances and differences between different philosophers, the Aristotelian idea of one eternal unmoved mover is perhaps the best example for the logic of classical theism.

5. Athenagoras's *A Plea for the Christians* points out that Christianity is of high moral standards (immorality was a common suspicion) and that Christians share their view of the unity of God with the Greek philosophers. See *Christian Classics Ethereal Library*, http://www.ccel.org/ccel /schaff/anf02.toc.html.

6. Justin Martyr, in his *First Apology*, notes that Christianity is not interested in a worldly kingdom, Ap. I,11. Christian Classics Ethereal Library, http://www.ccel.org/ccel/schaff/anf01/Page_166.html.

7. Klaus Wengst, *Pax Romana and the Peace of Jesus Christ*, trans. John Bowden (Philadelphia: Fortress Press, 1987), 2.

8. John Dominic Crossan, *Jesus: A Revolutionary Biography* (San Francisco: HarperSanFrancisco, 1994), 27, emphasis in original.

9. See, for instance, Neil Elliott, *Liberating Paul: The Justice of God and the Politics of the Apostle* (Maryknoll: Orbis Books, 1994), 197–98; and John Dominic Crossan and Jonathan L. Reed, *In Search of Paul: How Jesus's Apostle Opposed Rome's Empire with God's Kingdom* (San Francisco: HarperSanFrancisco, 2004), 235–36.

10. Blaming the poor for being lazy and at fault not only for their own situation but also for the state of the community is perhaps as old as poverty itself, yet it is especially troublesome under the conditions of empire, where inequalities are pronounced and growing, and where the power and wealth of some is built on the back of others.

11. In recent years, the Occupy Wall Street movement might serve as a case study. This movement did not simply disappear or fizzle out; this

movement was forcefully broken up by police forces in riot gear all around the country in November of 2011.

12. Daniel Burke, "Pope Suggests It's Better to Be an Atheist than a Bad Christian," *CNN*, February 24, 2017, http://www.cnn.com/2017/02/23/world/pope-atheists-again/index.html.

13. See Jillian Berman, "U.S. Income Inequality Higher than Roman Empire's Levels: Study," *Huffington Post*, December 19, 2011, http://www.huffingtonpost.com/2011/12/19/us-income-inequality-ancient-rome-levels_n_1158926.html.

14. The Arians, according to their critics, rejected the idea of Christ's divinity. In the past, this has often been seen as a liberal theological move. However, it could also be a conservative move, as by maintaining a single authority at the top they maintained the basic principle and power of the Roman Empire. See Rieger, *Christ and Empire*, chapter 2.

15. The earliest image of Christ as *pantocrator*—the ruler over all things—is thought to date from the sixth century, as is an image of Christ dressed in the military uniform of an emperor. For the earliest images of Christ, see https://www.coraevans.com/blog/article/here-are-the-10-oldest-images-of-christ.

16. For the term *deep solidarity*, see the conclusion below and Rieger and Kwok, *Occupy Religion*; and Rieger and Henkel-Rieger, *Unified We Are a Force*.

17. See Rieger, *Christ and Empire*, chapter 2. See also Jon Sobrino, *Jesus in Latin America* (Maryknoll: Orbis Books, 1987), 19–29.

18. Gregory of Nazianzus, "Third Theological Oration," *The Trinitarian Controversy*, ed. and trans. William Rusch (Philadelphia: Fortress Press, 1980), 132, concedes in his reflections on the doctrine of the Trinity that "monarchy is the opinion honored by us, yet a monarchy which one person does not determine," adding that this "is impossible for originated nature," and thus defusing the political challenge.

19. Neoliberal capitalism is characterized by deregulation of the economy (less government involvement), free trade, privatization, and the firm

(but unproven) conviction that if the wealthy are doing better, everyone is doing better, manifesting in tax cuts to the wealthy and to corporations and in a redirection of government subsidies to corporations ("too big to fail") rather than to communities and individuals in need. For a critique of the neoliberal capitalist assumption that a rising tide will lift all boats, see Joerg Rieger, *No Rising Tide: Theology, Economics, and the Future* (Minneapolis: Fortress Press, 2009).

20. Frederick Herzog, "Let Us Still Praise Famous Men," *Hannavee* 1 (April 1970): 6.

21. National Center for Children in Poverty, http://www.nccp.org /topics/childpoverty.html.

22. Ernst Bloch, *Atheismus im Christentum: Zur Religion des Exodus und des Reichs* (Frankfurt: Suhrkamp, 1968), 24.

23. See, for instance, Elsa Tamez, *The Amnesty of Grace: Justification by Faith from a Latin American Perspective,* trans. Sharon H. Ringe (Nashville: Abingdon Press, 1993); and Brigitte Kahl, *Galatians Re-Imagined*, 204–7.

24. Petronius, *Satyricon* 14:2, quoted in Wengst, *Pax Romana and the Peace of Jesus Christ*, 40.

25. Saki Knafo, "When It Comes to Illegal Drugs, White America Does the Crime, Black America Gets the Time," *Huffington Post*, September 17, 2013, http://www.huffingtonpost.com/2013/09/17/racial -disparity-drug-use_n_3941346.html. According to the ACLU, "Race and the Death Penalty," African Americans make up 55 percent of people on death row today and 43 percent of total executions since 1976. See https://www.aclu.org/other/race-and-death-penalty. See also Ava Duvernay's critically acclaimed film, *13th*.

26. K. Koch, "sdq, gemeinschaftstreu/heilvoll sein," *Theologisches Handwörterbuch zum Alten Testament*, vol. 2, ed. Ernst Jenni and Claus Westermann (Munich and Zurich: Christian Kaiser Verlag, Theologischer Verlag Zürich, 1984), 507–30.

27. This is the point of Horsley, *Jesus and the Powers*.

2. GIVE TO CAESAR WHAT IS CAESAR'S AND TO GOD WHAT IS GOD'S

1. This did not happen by accident, of course. The Christian Right, supported by large amounts of money, has been organizing for decades. The history of the close link between conservative economics, politics, and religion is told by several authors. See, for instance, Kevin M. Kruse, *One Nation Under God: How Corporate America Invented Christian America* (New York: Basic Books, 2015).

2. For the contemporary situation, see Robert S. McElvaine, *Grand Theft Jesus: The Hijacking of Religion in America* (New York: Crown Publishers, 2008).

3. Carol Hanisch, "The Personal Is Political," *Notes from the Second Year: Women's Liberation*, ed. Shulamith Firestone and Anne Koedt (New York: Radical Feminism: 1970).

4. Charles Villa-Vicencio, *Between Christ and Caesar: Classic and Contemporary Texts on Church and State* (Cape Town and Grand Rapids: David Philip and William B. Eerdmans Publishing Company, 1986), xxi. The author continues that the church's "noblest tradition is one of undaunted decision making." Describing the South African situation toward the end of the book, Villa-Vicencio distinguishes periods of alignment of church and state, resistance, and finally initiative, beginning with a decision of the World Alliance of Reformed Churches to declare apartheid a heresy (197–205).

5. See, for instance, the efforts of the late Reverend Jerry Falwell's "Moral Majority" and the Reverend Pat Robertson's "Christian Coalition of America."

6. For this interpretation, which has become increasingly prominent, see Horsley, *Jesus and the Powers*, 175. He also notes that Jesus's declaration was not a call to arms but a declaration of independence from Rome.

7. De La Torre, *The Politics of Jesús*, 29.

8. See also the nuanced interpretation of this passage by Wengst, *Pax Romana and the Peace of Jesus Christ*, 58–61. Recent postcolonial and

decolonial readings of the Bible have emphasized the ambiguity of the Bible. Some see Jesus's response to paying taxes as one example of this ambiguity (Sugirtharajah, *Postcolonial Criticism and Biblical Interpretation*, 89–90), as Jesus could have addressed the problem in more straightforward ways. However, when the status quo is built on certainty and the lack of ambiguity, the challenge that is presented here should not be underestimated, and neither should be the dangers and the questionable success of open opposition. Recall that Jesus was dangerous enough to get killed on a Roman Cross.

9. *The United Methodist Book of Resolutions*, "White Privilege in the United States," http://www.umc.org/what-we-believe/white-privilege-in-the-united-states. The Presbyterian Church USA adopted a confession on the topic at its 44th General Assembly in 2016: http://byfaithonline.com/wp-content/uploads/2016/06/Overture-43-clean.pdf. See also the United States Conference of Catholic Bishops, which published a set of resources titled "Responding to the Sin of Racism," http://www.usccb.org/issues-and-action/cultural-diversity/african-american/resources/upload/Responding-to-the-Sin-of-Racism-USCCB-Resource.pdf.

10. James Cone, *A Black Theology of Liberation*, 2nd ed. (Maryknoll: Orbis Books, 1986), 119–28.

11. Frederick Herzog, *Liberation Theology: Liberation in the Light of the Fourth Gospel* (New York: Seabury Press, 1972), 62–63.

12. See the following resources: https://en.wikipedia.org/wiki/Economics_of_the_Roman_army; https://www.nationalpriorities.org/campaigns/military-spending-united-states/; https://www.nationalpriorities.org/campaigns/us-military-spending-vs-world/.

13. Horsley, *Jesus and the Powers*, 26–31.

14. Wengst, *Pax Romana and the Peace of Jesus Christ*, 56–58.

15. Horsley, *Jesus and the Powers*, 79–80.

16. Keep in mind, as pointed out in chapter 1, that 21 percent of children in the United States are living below the poverty line and

43 percent in near-poverty conditions. This is the case even though most of their parents are working, often more than one job.

17. The term *corporate welfare* refers, tongue-in-cheek, to the fact that while government spending is commonly scrutinized and criticized when it comes to welfare for people in need, large corporations receive substantial amounts of government subsidies and other benefits.

18. John Maxfield, "A Foolish Take: The Modern History of U.S. Corporate Income Taxes," *USA Today*, January 2, 2018, https://www .usatoday.com/story/money/markets/2017/12/30/a-foolish-take-the -modern-history-of-us-corporate-income-taxes/108925604/. From 1952– 1963, the corporate tax rate was at its highest, at 53 percent.

19. See Ralph Nader, *Only the Super-Rich Can Save Us!* (New York: Seven Stories Press, 2009).

20. The populations of the Americas were reduced by as much as 90 percent following the various colonization projects, decreasing the population from 100 million to 10 million. This amounts to "the most demographic disaster…in human history." Some historians point to diseases as a major factor but fail to account for economic pressures that left populations more vulnerable to disease than they would have otherwise been. See Roxanne Dunbar-Ortiz, "Yes, Native Americans Were the Victims of Genocide," *Truthout*, June 4, 2016, http://www.truth-out.org/opinion /item/36257-yes-native-americans-were-the-victims-of-genocide.

21. For the European colonizers of the eighteenth and nineteenth centuries, Las Casas was considered the hero.

22. Rieger, *Christ and Empire*, chapter 4.

23. Bartolomé de las Casas, *The Only Way*, ed. Helen Rand Parish, trans. Francis Patrick Sullivan, S.J. (New York: Paulist Press, 1992), 68, 93.

24. John Howard Yoder, *The Politics of Jesus: Vicit Agnus Noster* (Grand Rapids: William B. Eerdmans, 1972), 46, promotes the notion of servanthood. Yoder claims that the sovereignty of the dominant powers must be broken and argues that Jesus did so by accepting his submission (147).

For the complexity of Yoder's legacy, including his own abuse of others, see Hilary Scarsella, "Not Making Sense: Why Stanley Hauerwas's Response to Yoder's Sexual Abuse Misses the Mark," *The Mennonite*, December 4, 2017, https://themennonite.org/feature/not-making-sense-stanley -hauerwass-response-yoders-sexual-abuse-misses-mark/.

25. The Greek term for brothers and sisters is *adelphoi,* translated in the NRSV as *students.*

26. Horsley, *Jesus and the Powers*, 53.

27. For the time of Jesus, see Horsley, *Jesus and the Powers*, 156. He notes that popular resistance does not have to be outright revolt.

28. In a conversation with students and colleagues, the Reverend James Lawson, one of the engineers of violent resistance in the civil rights movement, reminded us of the profound difference between generic ideas of nonviolence and the particular methods of nonviolent resistance. Conversation in Dallas, Texas, September 2013.

29. On Jesus ben Hananiah, see Horsley, *Jesus and Empire*, 51, 129. Yoder, *The Politics of Jesus*, 59, notes that the Jewish and Roman authorities were protecting themselves against a real threat, which he takes as evidence for the political relevance of nonviolent tactics.

30. Yoder, *The Politics of Jesus*, 34, observes that language like *kingdom of God* and *good news* is chosen from the political realm. Without needing to agree in detail what Jesus's politics looks like—Yoder's interpretation presents but one option—it is clear that Jesus's ministry has political implications that counter the politics of the dominant system.

31. See Wengst, *Pax Romana and the Peace of Jesus Christ*, 55.

32. Alfred Loisy, *The Gospel and the Church*, trans. Christopher Home (Philadelphia: Fortress Press, 1976), 166.

33. Crossan, *Jesus: A Revolutionary Biography*, 55.

34. https://hymnary.org/text/ive_a_crown_up_in_the_kingdom. Another example is the slaves' appropriation of Charles Wesley's hymn "Roll Jordan, Roll," where the phrase "sitting in the kingdom" is used. Images

of the Jordan were often references to the Mississippi River and the escape to freedom from the bonds of slavery.

35. This is the limitation of much of recent scholarship that has otherwise helped to deepen our understanding of Jesus. See, for instance, Crossan, *Jesus: A Revolutionary Biography*, 56–58, presenting Jesus as teaching revolutionary wisdom as an "illiterate peasant, but with an oral brilliance that few of those trained in literate and scribal disciplines can ever attain" (58).

36. Jesus as an organizer is a recurring theme in Horsley, *Jesus and the Powers*. Yoder, *The Politics of Jesus*, 40, reminds us of the importance of the Jesus movement because new teachings in themselves are no threat if the teacher is an individual.

37. Horsley, *Jesus and the Powers*, 78–80.

38. Note the long history of religion and labor in the United States that today is too often forgotten. For one study see Heath W. Carther, *Union Made: Working People and the Rise of Social Christianity in Chicago* (New York: Oxford University Press, 2015).

39. See Gerhard Lohfink, *Jesus and Community: The Social Dimension of Christian Faith*, trans. John P. Galvin (Philadelphia and New York: Fortress Press and Paulist Press, 1984), 122–32. This contrast society is deeply rooted in ancient Jewish traditions, according to which "the people's conduct must correspond to the liberating action of God who chose Israel from all nations and saved it from Egypt" (123).

40. Friedrich Schleiermacher, the father of liberal theology, constructs his Christology in terms of the dichotomy of coercion and attraction, arguing that Christ embodies the latter. Nevertheless, despite a critique of missionary coercion, Schleiermacher's notion of attraction maintains colonial traits of superiority. See Rieger, *Christ and Empire*, chapter 5.

41. See Néstor Míguez, Joerg Rieger, and Jung Mo Sung, *Beyond the Spirit of Empire: Theology and Politics in a New Key* (London: SCM Press, 2009), chapter 5.

42. Theodore W. Jennings, *Transforming Atonement: A Political Theology of the Cross* (Minneapolis: Fortress Press, 2009), 216, puts it best:

"Without such a new God or new understanding of God, there can be no new politics, no final overcoming of the structures of division and domination, no democracy to come, no reign of justice and generosity and joy."

43. This is a term coined by Ada-María Isasi-Díaz, *Mujerista Theology* (Maryknoll: Orbis Books, 1996), 89, in order to deconstruct the hierarchical language implied in the term *kingdom*. However, in a patriarchal society, even the term *kin-dom* is limited.

3. THE MATERIALISM OF RELIGION

1. World Health Organization, *Climate Change and Health*, July 2017, http://www.who.int/mediacentre/factsheets/fs266/en/.

2. John Cook, et al., "Consensus on Consensus: A Synthesis on Consensus Estimates on Human-Caused Global Warming," *Environmental Research Letters* 11:4, April 13, 2016, http://iopscience.iop.org/article/10.1088/1748-9326/11/4/048002. This article notes a 97 percent consensus among actively publishing climate scientists that climate change is linked to human activity.

3. Sarah Iles Johnston, "Mysteries," *Ancient Religions*, ed. Sarah Iles Johnston (Cambridge: Belknap Press and Harvard University Press, 2007), 98–111. The Emperor Julian, for instance, in office from 361–363 CE, was initiated into three different mystery religions.

4. The books of the Left Behind series by Tim LaHaye and Jerry B. Jenkins that promote this interpretation rank high among history's best-sellers.

5. For an extended argument, see Joerg Rieger, *No Rising Tide: Theology, Economics, and the Future* (Minneapolis: Fortress Press, 2009), chapter 4.

6. Horsley, *Jesus and the Powers*, 93.

7. See Horsley, *Jesus and the Powers*, 100–101.

8. Attributed to Pierre Teilhard de Chardin.

9. Albert Schweitzer, *The Quest of the Historical Jesus*, first complete edition, ed. John Bowden (Minneapolis: Fortress Press, 2001).

10. John Wesley, Sermon "The Scripture Way of Salvation," *The Bicentennial Edition of the Works of John Wesley*, vol. 2, ed. Albert C. Outler (Nashville: Abingdon Press, 1985), 153–69.

11. Friedrich Schleiermacher, the father of liberal theology, is the example. In his work, there is a strict division of labor between Jesus and God in terms of private/communal and public/political. See Rieger, *Christ and Empire*, chapter 5.

12. Neither is the notion of the rapture very old. It only achieved popularity in the nineteenth century.

13. De La Torre, *The Politics of Jesús*, 130: "Those who are already humble need not hear more sermons advocating humility."

14. This is the so-called Mosaic covenant. See Horsley, *Jesus and the Powers*, 131. Horsley, ibid., 133, notes that the villages practiced a certain amount of mutual cooperation and reciprocity.

15. Horsley, *Jesus and the Powers*, 142, points out that the only way to become rich was to defraud the vulnerable.

16. Attributed to Kenyan Prime Minister and President Jomo Kenyatta, though often misattributed to South African Archbishop Desmond Tutu.

17. See the work of George Tinker, *Missionary Conquest: The Gospel and Native American Genocide* (Minneapolis: Fortress Press, 1993).

18. John Wesley, "On the Present Scarcity of Provisions," *The Works of John Wesley* (Jackson), vol. 11, 3rd ed. (Peabody, MA: Hendrickson Publishers, 1986), 54–55, worries that almost half the grain produced in England was used in the production of alcohol.

19. John Wesley, Sermon "Upon Our Lord's Sermon on the Mount: Discourse the Eighth," *The Bicentennial Edition of the Works of John Wesley*, vol. 1, 629.

20. De La Torre, *The Politics of Jesús*, 118.

21. In Latin American liberation theology, the conversation has always included the notion of the "crucified people." See, for instance, Jon Sobrino, *Where Is God? Earthquake, Terrorism, Barbarity, and Hope*, trans. Margaret Wilde (Maryknoll: Orbis Books, 2004).

22. Horsley, *Jesus and the Powers*, 199–200, notes that the crucifixion resulted in a breakthrough that helped the Jesus movement advance and increase the challenge to the Roman Empire, linked to energy that was produced by Jesus's confrontation with the rulers.

23. This insight is deeply embedded in many contemporary resistance traditions. For a take on the cross by an African American labor leader, listen to A. Philip Randolph: "The law of the achievement of freedom, justice and equality is the law of the Seed and the Cross. This is the law of struggle, sacrifice, suffering. It is the law of death. Death precedes life. The seed must decay and die before the tree can live. Jesus Christ had to bear the cross and die in order to give life everlasting. Verily, there is no royal road to freedom." Quoted in Cynthia Taylor, *A. Phillip Randolph: The Religious Journey of an African American Labor Leader* (New York: New York University Press, 2006), 162. In the field of theology, the suffering of God with Jesus on the cross was one of the crucial insights of Jürgen Moltmann, *The Crucified God: The Cross as the Foundation and Criticism of Christian Theology*, trans. R. A. Wilson and John Bowden (New York: Harper and Row, 1974). Note that this does not have to amount to the problems of Patripassianism, a position that claimed that the experience of the first person of the trinity was identical to the second.

24. This can be seen early on, for instance, in the work of Marcion (85–160 CE). Certain modern definitions of religion as a nonpolitical and private matter display similar characteristics.

25. N. T. Wright, "Paul's Gospel and Caesar's Empire," *Paul and Politics: Ekklesia, Israel, Imperium, Interpretation*, ed. Richard Horsley (Harrisburg: Trinity Press International, 2000), 182, has argued that Paul should be taught as much in political science departments as in religious studies departments.

26. A postcolonial interpreter, Stephen Moore, "Mark and Empire: 'Zealot' and 'Postcolonial' Readings," *Postcolonial Theologies: Divinity and Empire*, ed. Catherine Keller, Michael Nausner, and Mayra Rivera (St. Louis: Chalice Press, 2004), 141, emphasizes the ambivalent attitudes of Mark toward the Roman Empire in this passage. Yet it is not necessary to claim Mark's full-blown resistance, as according to the work of Homi Bhabha, ambivalence presents substantial challenges to empires who seek to control everything.

27. Horsley, *Jesus and the Powers*, 110, notes the difference between acts of power and miracles or magic (which depend on the distinction between natural and supernatural). The point of these acts of power is not the transgression of nature but resistance against alien-possessing forces. See also Ched Myers, *Binding the Strong Man: A Political Reading of Mark's Story of Jesus* (Maryknoll: Orbis Books, 1988), 436, who adds that of Jesus's miracles the exorcisms were what was most threatening to the political authorities.

28. This is the motto of the World Social Forum.

29. This is the way in which Karl Barth, who has often been seen as the quintessential theologian of transcendence, interprets Jesus Christ. Transcendence is found in the manger, not in the sky. Karl Barth, *Dogmatics in Outline* (New York: Harper and Row, 1959), 40, notes that the highness of God consists in God's descent into the "utter depths of the existence of his creature" in Jesus Christ.

30. Feminist theologians have noted problems with the notion of love, as it conjures up stereotypes of feminine self-giving and sacrifice. For an alternative take on love from an American-Korean feminist perspective see Wonhee Anne Joh, *Heart of the Cross: A Postcolonial Christology* (Louisville: Westminster John Knox, 2006). See also Barbara E. Reid, O.P., *Taking Up the Cross: New Testament Interpretations through Latina and Feminist Eyes* (Minneapolis: Fortress Press, 2007).

31. Horsley argues that Jesus's bringing them together is a "bold innovation" (*Jesus and the Powers*, 149).

4. GOD VS. MAMMON

1. See chapter 1.

2. United Nations, Human Development Report (New York: Oxford University Press, 1998), 30. For the more recent statistics, see Oxfam, https://www.oxfam.org/en/pressroom/pressreleases/2017-01-16/just-8 -men-own-same-wealth-half-world.

3. See chapter 1.

4. As noted earlier, deregulation, free enterprise, and the hope that if the wealthy are doing better everyone will be doing better are key trademarks of neoliberal capitalism.

5. For an emerging conversation on matters of religion and class see *Religion, Theology, and Class: Fresh Engagements after Long Silence*, ed. Joerg Rieger (New York: Palgrave Macmillan, 2013). For an exploration of class in the thought of the Apostle Paul see L. L. Welborn, "Marxism and Capitalism in Pauline Studies," *Paul and Economics: A Handbook*, ed. Thomas R. Blanton IV and Raymond Pickett (Minneapolis: Fortress Press, 2017), 361–96.

6. For the historical background of the following account, see Horsley, *Jesus and the Powers*, 26–37, 134–35.

7. For the broader context, see critical examinations of the invention and fetishization of currency like Richard Seaford's *Money and the Early Greek Mind: Homer, Philosophy, Tragedy* (New York: Cambridge University Press, 2004).

8. In a court ruling of the Michigan Supreme Court in 1919 (*Dodge v. Ford Motor Company*), the brothers John Francis Dodge and Horace Elgin Dodge, owners of 10 percent of Ford stock, challenged Ford's decision to cut dividends in order to invest in new plants and grow production and numbers of workers, while cutting prices. The court ruled in favor of the Dodge brothers, arguing that a corporation is organized primarily for the profit of its stockholders rather than for the benefit of its employees or for the community. See also the brief entry in Wikipedia, "Dodge

v. Ford Motor Company," http://en.wikipedia.org/wiki/Dodge_v._Ford_Motor_Company.

9. See also Isaiah 3:13-15.

10. Kim Bobo, *Wage Theft in America: Why Millions of Americans Are Not Getting Paid and What We Can Do About It* (New York: New Press, 2009).

11. For an extended engagement with this theory and its representatives, see Rieger, *No Rising Tide*.

12. See Brent Waters, *Just Capitalism: A Christian Ethic of Economic Globalization* (Louisville: Westminster John Knox, 2016).

13. The topic of the sacrifices required by capitalism have been discussed at length in Latin American liberation theology. See, for instance, Franz Hinkelammert, *The Ideological Weapons of Death: A Theological Critique of Capitalism*, trans. Philip Berryman (Maryknoll: Orbis Books, 1986); and Jung Mo Sung, *Desire, Market, and Religion*, Reclaiming Liberation Theology (London: SCM Press, 2007).

14. See Rieger, *No Rising Tide*, 86–87.

15. For the topic of poverty at the time of Jesus, particularly in Galilee, see Sakari Häkinnen, "Poverty in the First-Century Galilee," *HTS Teologiese Studies/HTS Theological Studies* 72:4, September 2016, http://www.scielo.org.za/pdf/hts/v72n4/46.pdf. At subsistence level or sometimes below were 40 percent of the population, 28 percent were below subsistence level (3). In comparison, as many as half of all residents in the United States live in or near poverty today. Paul Buchheit, "Yes, Half of Americans Are In or Near Poverty: Here's More Evidence," *Common Dreams*, October 16, 2017, https://www.commondreams.org/views/2017/10/16/yes-half-americans-are-or-near-poverty-heres-more-evidence.

16. While John has often been interpreted as an anti-Semitic Gospel, the Johannine community hardly challenges all Jews in general or all Jewish people; the challenge is directed, instead, to certain powerful elites. See, for instance, Teresa Okure, "John," *The International Bible Commentary*,

ed. William Farmer (Collegeville, MN: Liturgical Press, 1990), 1446, who also reminds us that, according to John 4:22, "salvation is from the Jews."

17. See Michael D. Yates, *Why Unions Matter* (New York: Monthly Review Press, 2009), 141–67.

18. Wengst, *Pax Romana and the Peace of Jesus Christ*, 62.

19. The notion of deep solidarity is developed further in Rieger and Henkel-Rieger, *Unified We Are a Force*.

20. One of the fathers of neoliberal capitalism, Milton Friedman, considered 6 percent "the natural rate of unemployment." His 1976 Nobel Prize was based in part on his study of the underlying phenomenon. See also https://www.nobelprize.org/nobel_prizes/economic-sciences /laureates/1976/press.html.

21. De La Torre also notes that from this perspective the employer has a moral responsibility toward the workers that goes beyond capitalist economics (*The Politics of Jesús*, 103–4).

22. The Social Principles of The United Methodist Church, introduction to paragraph 163. *The 2016 Book of Discipline of The United Methodist Church* (Nashville: The United Methodist Publishing House 2016), 131.

23. Néstor Míguez, *Jesús del Pueblo* (Buenos Aires: Ediciones Kairos, 2011), 107. Miguez also draws some parallels between the strategies of neoliberal capitalism and the Roman Empire, including privatization and a lack of influence of the people (105).

24. See the responses of Job to Eliphaz, Bildad, and Zophar throughout the book of Job.

25. For a user-friendly reading of the different stories told in Western culture to account for the status of the impoverished, see Alain de Botton's *Status Anxiety* (London: Hamish Hamilton, 2014).

26. Horsley, *Jesus and the Powers*, 87ff., 136.

27. See Leviticus 25. Whether or not the Jubilee Year initially was an effort of the privileged classes to diffuse economic tensions is debated, in

Jesus's message; however, this tradition is employed in the struggle against the Roman Empire. See the discussion in Jack Nelson-Pallmeyer, *Jesus Against Christianity: Reclaiming the Missing Jesus* (Harrisburg: Trinity Press International, 2001), 7–10.

28. See also Horsley, *Jesus and the Powers*, 139.

29. Wengst, *Pax Romana and the Peace of Jesus Christ*, 69.

30. For the notion of solidarity among working people, see Rieger and Henkel-Rieger, *Unified We Are a Force*.

31. One of the most successful campaigns during the height of the Occupy Wall Street movement was buying up student debt and then forgiving it. Shahien Nasiripour, "Occupy Buys, Then Cancels, Student Debt," *Huffington Post*, September 17, 2014, http://www.huffingtonpost .com/2014/09/17/occupy-wall-street-student-debt_n_5839174.html. See also: http://rollingjubilee.org/transparency/.

32. Wengst, *Pax Romana and the Peace of Jesus Christ*, 140.

33. De La Torre, *The Politics of Jesús*, 151.

34. Of course, we are not in a position to go back and restore the village communities that existed at the time of Jesus. Today, we might consider other options of economic communities, including cooperative business models where communal models of production empower all participants to have a say and determine fair and equitable distribution of the wealth produced. See, for instance, Richard D. Wolff, *Democracy at Work: A Cure for Capitalism* (Chicago: Haymarket Books, 2012), and the over sixty-year history of the Mondragon Corporation in Spain (https://www .mondragon-corporation.com/en/).

5. THE WAY, THE TRUTH, AND THE LIFE?

1. The contemporary shapes of some religious traditions were created after the model of imperial Christianity. See Tomoko Masuzawa, *The*

Invention of World Religions, Or, How European Universalism Was Preserved in the Language of Pluralism (Chicago: University of Chicago Press, 2005).

2. Rieger, *Christ and Empire*, chapter 4.

3. Wengst, *Pax Romana and the Peace of Jesus Christ*, 7–11; 21–22.

4. Christian interpreters, both Protestant and Roman Catholic, have emphasized the connection of truth and word in the narrow sense. See, for instance, Rudolf Schnackenburg, *Das Johannesevangelium*, vol. 2, 4th ed., *Herders Theologischer Kommentar zum Neuen Testament* (Freiburg: Herder, 1985), 280. This overlooks that for John the word is more than just the Bible or the words of Jesus; it is the reality of Jesus, as the word *(logos)* became flesh, according to John 1:14. This insight brings greater nuance and complexity to a reading of John 8:31.

5. The first line of this hymn is "Once to Every Man and Nation Comes the Moment to Decide." This is the opposite of the interpretation of Schnackenburg, *Das Johannesevangelium*, vol. 3, 72, who emphasizes the "hoheitliche Klang" (sovereign sound) and the dominant character of Jesus's statement.

6. This image can be found in the Archbishop's Chapel in Ravenna, Italy, which was built in 495 CE, https://en.wikipedia.org/wiki /Archbishop%27s_Chapel,_Ravenna.

7. For the notion of the multitude see Rieger and Kwok, *Occupy Religion*. One context in which this notion developed was Korean Minjung theology, interpreting the Gospel of Mark. See the work of the Korean theologian Ahn Byung-Mu and the discussion by Volker Küster, *Jesus und das Volk im Markusevangelium: Ein Beitrag zum interkulturellen Gespräch in der Exegese* (Neukirchen-Vluyn: Neukirchener Verlag, 1996).

8. See the Heidelberg Disputation of 1518, thesis 20. This is part of Luther's embrace of a "theology of the cross" in opposition to what he calls the "theology of glory," which is the expression of dominant Christianity. For a copy of the text see http://bookofconcord.org/heidelberg.php.

9. Ernst Käsemann, "The Canon of the New Testament and the Unity of the Church," *Ernst Käsemann, Essays on New Testament Themes*, trans. W. J. Montague (London: SCM Press, 1964), 103.

10. See Schnackenburg, who emphasizes the difference between Jewish and Hellenistic thought—basing his observations on the parallels between John and the Qumran communities but failing to consider the power differential (*Das Johannesevangelium*, vol. 2, 268).

11. Thanks to my colleague Santiago Slabodsky for this helpful distinction. In history, slavery is an example of forced inclusion, and genocide the most dramatic example of forced exclusion.

12. This includes even American Corporations, in particular IBM. See Edwin Black, *IBM and the Holocaust: The Strategic Alliance between Nazi Germany and America's Most Powerful Corporation* (New York: Crown Publishers, 2001).

13. Friedrich von Logau (1604–1655): "*In Gefahr und grosser Not führt der Mittelweg zum Tod.*"

14. This is the solution proposed by Mark A. Noll, *Adding Cross to Crown: The Political Significance of Christ's Passion* (Grand Rapids: Baker Books, 1996). Noll assumes that "within…basic biblical guidelines, the practicalities of a Christian politics alert to the cross may not differ all that much from a Christian politics inspired by the vision of the ruling Christ" (32).

15. See Colleen M. Conway's description of the anti-Judaism implied in the Gospel of John, synagogue expulsion hypotheses, and the rise of supersessionist readings of this Gospel in *John and the Johannine Letters* (Nashville: Abingdon Press, 2017), 5–6, 39–49, 109ff.

16. See Rieger, *Christ and Empire*, chapters 4 and 5.

17. Ibid., chapter 5.

18. Tinker, *Missionary Conquest*.

19. See José Míguez Bonino, "Methodism and Latin American Liberation Movements," *Methodist and Radical: Rejuvenating Tradition*, ed. Joerg Rieger and John Vincent (Nashville: Kingswood Books, 2003), 193–206.

20. Míguez, *The Practice of Hope*, 182.

21. See chapter 1.

22. See chapter 1.

23. See the interpretation of Ulrich Luz, *Das Evangelium des Matthäus* vol. I/1, 5th ed., *Evangelisch-Katholischer Kommentar zum Neuen Testament* (Düsseldorf and Neukirchen-Vluyn: Benziger Verlag and Neukirchener Verlag, 2002), 454. Luz lists the parallels to the Shemoneh-Esrei prayer.

24. This is the deeply problematic approach of Samuel P. Huntington, *The Clash of Civilizations and the Remaking of the World Order* (New York: Touchstone, 1997).

25. For faith and the Occupy Wall Street movement see Rieger and Kwok, *Occupy Religion*.

26. Rudolf Bultmann, *Das Evangelium des Johannes*, 16th ed., *Kritisch-exegetischer Kommentar über das Neue Testament* (Göttingen: Vandenhoeck und Ruprecht, 1959), interpretation of John 14:6. Regarding the person of faith, Bultmann says, "sein Weg ist schon sein Ziel" (467); "im Gehen des Weges ist das Ziel erreicht" (468); truth is only found in walking, "im Gehen" (469).

27. Reinhold Niebuhr, "The Serenity Prayer": "God, grant me the serenity to accept the things I cannot change, / Courage to change the things I can, / And wisdom to know the difference."

28. Obery M. Hendricks, *The Politics of Jesus: Rediscovering the True Revolutionary Nature of Jesus' Teachings and How They Have Been Corrupted* (New York: Doubleday, 2006), 326–27, notes that in the Gospel of Mark in particular Jesus is characterized as being on the way, setting the "kingdom in motion" by his "words and deeds." For an interpretation of Judaism and Christianity as religions on the road see Joerg Rieger, *Faith on the Road: A Short Theology of Travel and Justice* (Downers Gove, IL: IVP Academic, 2015).

CONCLUSION

1. These are no doubt central to Christian faith and deep symbols of sacred power at work in human relationships.

2. That's what Jesus seems to be saying in Luke 23:34: "Father forgive them; for they do not know what they are doing," a statement that is missing in some ancient versions of Luke. But do the powerful, including Caesar, really not know what they are doing? While individuals may experience pardon, we cannot let the principalities of powers off the hook. Otherwise the crucifixions will continue, as they have in many forms throughout the centuries.

3. Some assume that the problem is individuals—racist police officers or deranged shooters—and others argue for more systemic measures, like body cameras for officers or gun control for the general public. What is often left open, though, is the question of what structures are at work here.

4. Wengst, *Pax Romana and the Peace of Jesus Christ*, 27.

5. See also Horsley, *Jesus and Empire*, 70

6. Anselm of Canterbury, *Proslogion*, in *Anselm of Canterbury: The Major Works* (Oxford: Oxford University Press, 1998), 87–88.

7. See Rieger, *Christ and Empire*, chapter 3.

8. See chapter 4.

9. See some of the stories of working people in Rieger and Henkel-Rieger, *Unified We Are a Force*.

10. Horsley, *Jesus and Empire*, 91. The so-called "Q source" refers to what might have been an ancient collection of sayings of Jesus that has been lost. Material from this source is found in the Gospels of Matthew and Luke but not Mark or John.

11. We are the 1 percent. We stand with the 99 percent. http:// westandwiththe99percent.tumblr.com.

INDEX

147